Cont

T0013228

Introduction

Military life boasts of travel to exotic places, immersion in the worldly cultures and cuisine that most Americans can only dream about . . . and on the government's dime, to boot!

At least, that's what the common perception is. But those who have served know that while the above may be true, military life comes with its own set of challenges and can be a hardship as much as it is rewarding.

Here to help is the advice, guidance, and personal stories of spouses from all walks of life, in stages from the newlywed to the retired and properly salty. They share tips on overcoming the numerous obstacles, and navigating the special culture, traditions, and the one-of-a-kind lingo of military service.

Gathered mostly from those who are affiliated with the military, but also from those with similar diplomatic lifestyles, the anecdotes reveal the special bond they share with their fellow spouses, and the wisdom gained to pass to the next generation.

The very special illustrations were created by a talented Air Force wife, and reflect both the strong beauty and earnestness of those who are engaged in our nation's most serious business, and yet, have learned to not take themselves too seriously.

PART 1

Annoying Acronyms and Other Gibberish

OH, FUN! MORE THINGS TO LEARN!

Where do I start? When you receive orders to move, you will have one million things to figure out. The first is how to read those orders. HHE, UAB, PCS, THA, to name just a few. But basically these all have to do with your life, your belongings, where they are going, and how they are going to get there.

These are things you need to know. These are things you often have to figure out for yourself. It also doesn't help that every branch/agency has their own variation of these, their own way of saying the same thing.

Once you figure these out, don't worry—*there are more*—and they will keep coming. Your spouse will start speaking in this abbreviated language and you'd better learn the lingo to be able to keep up. Who knows, you may be fluent soon. You can also try creating your own acronyms to keep him on his toes and have some fun of your own.

—Victoria Griffith

ALPHABET SOUP

When joining the military community, you must learn the recipe for alphabet soup as you will be inundated by acronyms from day one. The good news is that now, Millennials and Gen Z have their own unique new words and phrases and will likely acclimate to this recipe quickly. As a young spouse decades ago with no military affiliation prior to my marriage, I often botched the recipe!

The first hack is to not be easily fooled by what you think you know, and the second hack is to know where the official "recipe books" are.

Hack 1: When encountering acronyms in military information, don't be fooled by those that seem familiar or that you think you understand. The alphabet recipe changes with time and has been influenced with the development of new equipment, operations or programs, or unique military humor. A few examples follow.

- **BZ** is known as a naval signal *Bravo Zulu*, or *well done!* It can also mean *Buffer Zone* and is the name of more than one commercial activity. It can also stand for *below the zone*—or early promotion in rank.
- **CC** in my world always meant to copy a designated person on an email or document. A person on my team recounted a story that she received a message to send the message to *CC*. She was baffled and asked the colonel she worked for to identify all those to be copied on the message. The colonel did not reply to her question and suggested that she immediately learn military terms. In this case it meant *Command & Control*. Big botch!
- Etsy and Pinterest have *DIY* projects; the military acronym for *do-it-yourself* is **DITY**, most commonly used for a *DITY move*. A *DITY move* seems like a good idea, but trust me—it is not!
- We all have our *FAVs* that we like on social media or mark with hearts in our digital photo albums, but the military **FAV** is a *fast attack vehicle*.

- Then there is **HUD** which we all know is the *Department of Housing and Urban Development.* Not so in the military or in some new cars! It is a *head up display.*
- Lastly, my favorite which I have used in my work many times to tell my team about a new hot task—a **GOBI**—a *general officer bright idea*! I find this acronym to be appropriately expressive with the perfect hint of sarcasm. Its civilian meaning is a South Asian dish or a desert in East Asia.

I could go on and on, but you get the **GIST** (*Graphical Intelligence Support Terminal*).

Hack 2: Recognize that the alphabet soup changes constantly. It's best to have a good recipe book for the soup. While Google will always serve up many choices for you, some of which are infused with military humor and quite fun, a few official sources exist that are helpful:

- MilitaryOneSource.mil
- Defense.gov
- jcs.mil/Portals/36/Documents/Doctrine/pubs/dictionary.pdf

Enjoy the alphabet soup and add a few ingredients of your own!

—*GamGam*

PT vs PT, RSO VS RSO, EFM VS EFM—LEARN TO ASK!

Nobody wants to look foolish or unknowledgeable. Acronyms undefined can lead to huge misunderstandings. The first time I discovered this was when my now-husband and I were dating.

Geographically separate, we talked on the phone in the evenings. I was working in the medical field and he was stationed halfway across the country. For what seemed like several months, he had been talking about going to PT. One night, he informed me the next day he would be playing football for PT. I lost my temper and demanded to know his physician's name as this was a clear case of malpractice!

Anyone in PT for months on end being told to play football was unbelievable! This is how I learned that "PT" in the military means "physical training" and not "physical therapy."

This would not be the last time I had to bring the conversation to a halt in order to get clarification. In certain assignments, an "EFM" is an "eligible" not "exceptional" family member and means you can get a job and not that you need special services.

Just this past fall, I discovered that although I have worked in the "RSO" (Regional Security Office) the acronym on a military base means "Religious Services Organization." Acronyms can differ in every branch, assignment, location, or culture and be influenced by current pop culture. When in doubt, ask!

—*Diana Ringquist*

A FEW IMPORTANT AND LESSER-KNOWN ACRONYMS AND ABBREVIATIONS

CAC: Common Access Card, also commonly referred to as the CAC, is a smart card about the size of a credit card that is used as identification in secure environments.

COC: Change of Command Ceremony, usually laden with snacks.

CONUS: Continental United States, the forty-eight connected states.

DEERS: Defense Enrollment Eligibility Reporting System, the tracking system for eligibility for health and other benefits.

DODEA: Department of Defense Education Activity. A school system for military and federal government civilian children in places such as overseas, where the local system lacks sufficient capacity, doesn't teach in English, or otherwise cannot meet their needs.

EAA: Employee Activity Association store is a small commissary/shoppette, such as at an embassy. The EAA also runs cafeteria/kitchens.

FRG: Family Readiness Group. During the Gulf War, the informal spouse networks were found to be so critical for families dealing with deployments that the system was made a formal and mandatory part of each service's programs. Every unit has an FRG, usually run by volunteers, but supported by professional DoD (Department of Defense) staff as well as a myriad of programs and official websites.

HHG (HHE): Household Goods. All your worldly possessions that are eligible to be packed up and moved. Always subject to a weight limit, and also restrictions due to various rules and customs, both of the service, and at your destination.

Last Four: the last four numbers of your sponsor's social security account number. It will be used to identify you for a number of services. It is best to memorize his/her entire SSA number; you will need it frequently.

LTS: Long Term Storage—stuff you need to say goodbye to for the length of your next assignment.

OCONUS: Outside the Continental US—all foreign countries, plus Alaska, Hawaii, and US Territories. In other words, anywhere except the forty-eight contiguous states.

OPSEC: Operational Security. Maintaining an awareness for keeping certain sensitive information secure. For example, spouses shouldn't discuss troop movements with anyone outside the unit/immediate family.

PCS: Permanent Change of Station—to a civilian: "moving." Related to ...

Space A: Space available—for things like military flights, or reservations at military hotels, the reservation system is structured so that priority goes to mission essential, or people on orders first; then there is a pecking order, active duty first, then families of active duty, then retirees/reserves, etc.

TDY: Temporary Duty. An assignment usually lasting six months or less, so not "Permanent." The family may or may not move, depending on circumstances.

THA: Temporary Housing Assistance/Allowance. A monetary allotment you are paid for living costs when you are traveling, or waiting for housing.

Tricare: The health insurance program for military family members, retirees, and retiree families.

UAB: Unaccompanied Baggage. Important stuff you send ahead to your new duty station, that you will need right away. However, sometimes it arrives at the same time, or not much before the rest of your HHG.

PART 2

Military Traditions–The Fun, The Ugly, and The Just Plain Confusing

KNOW YOUR ROLE

My most memorable Army tradition FAIL comes after just one year of marriage, most of which was spent with my husband deployed. He came home in April of 2008, and I immediately became pregnant. It wasn't three months later when he was to be promoted to interim commander.

There is usually a Change of Command Ceremony (COC) when they take command and he had told me nothing about when it was, or any other details.

I remember asking, "Do I need to do anything for this?"

His response was, "No, babe."

Silly me, I believed him.

He came home one morning after PT and said, "Come on, we have to go!"

What?! Remember I said I was pregnant? The only things that fit were a pair of jeans and a white t-shirt. I kid you not. Not only was I expected to be at the COC, and had a special seat under the tent, but I was also supposed to *provide food and drinks* for the reception after it!

Never have I ever been so embarrassed in front of such a large group of people. And never was there such a large group of spouses, soldiers, and officers so hungry!

LIFE HACK

Make sure you ask some other spouses about what the expectations are for you. Your military spouse will be concentrating on his or her own role.

—*Katie Elze*

STANDING TALL AGAINST THE (SOMETIMES) PREVAILING STEREOTYPES

If the Military wanted you to have a family,
they would have issued you one.
—OLD PROVERB

After waiting two hours with my newborn son in my arms, my service member's "last four" (last four numbers of the sponsor's social security number) were called and I gathered my things and followed the gentleman into his office. Less than five minutes later, I was told that I could not register my son in the DEERS program without my service member being with me, because I "could not prove the child exists" despite my offer to change his now-dirty diaper on the man's desk. I left the office, newborn son still unregistered and my temper flaring.

Being a military spouse carries with it plenty of stereotypes—sadly, most of them are negative. Whether you became a military spouse shortly after graduating school or joined after years of holding down a high-powered and lucrative career, the entry into the ranks of military spouse can be jarring.

The way in which spouses are treated varies by branch and service member rank. One thing that seems to remain consistent is the idea that "you aren't the Service Member and therefore you can't . . ." It can be extremely difficult to come to terms with the fact that the rules are the rules, they are different for you and your spouse, and regardless of how offensive or cumbersome you may find them, they are no reflection on you as a person.

Getting involved in your FRG (Family Readiness Group), your community, and your spouse organizations can help you find support and provide you with a part in the collective voice in order to change how we are treated for the better.

—Diana Ringquist

WHY ARE THEY ALL DRESSED LIKE THAT?

"Why are all these women dressed in frilly, lacey dresses?" I quietly asked my future brother-in-law.

"Because the men like to see them looking pretty and soft when they come in from the field," he replied.

"I'm never going to fit in, am I?" I asked as I adjusted my powerful, classically cut, professional pant suit.

"Nope. Never."

Fitting in with your new community can go smoothly as most military communities are welcoming and reach out to offer you support and assistance as you settle in. Not all do this well, unfortunately, for the new arrivals. When you enter a new community, you may find yourself to be a square peg. This can be painful, and you may feel isolated.

General wisdom will advise you to get out and get involved to make new friends. As an extrovert, you may find this exciting. If you are an introvert or a naturally shy person, you may opt for climbing Mount Everest in a bikini as an easier option.

Be easy on yourself and be who you are. You may need to stretch yourself out of your comfort zone in order to meet others and make connections. It is rare that your new best friend will simply come looking for you. If you have questions, ask. Access your creativity and find ways to connect and participate in your community. I was asked to write hacks for this book, after all!

—Diana Ringquist

ROOF STOMPS 101

My introduction to a roof stomp was one of the coolest party-time events I have ever experienced. Entering into my role as a "serious girlfriend" to my hot fighter-pilot beau, I found myself scaling a ladder up to the roof of the Brigadier General Wing Commander's residence at 01:00 on a Saturday morning.

Expecting to be taken away by Security Forces, we were instead greeted with smiling faces, lots of beer, and what I would learn to be the legendary casserole of Eggtopia! Eggtopia consists of whatever is in the refrigerator mixed with eggs and cheese ... and tastes fabulous with beer and a party.

View from our front door. "0 Dark 30," April 2010, Misawa, Japan. 14th FS, The Fightin' Samurai.

Fast forward to thirteen years later, my husband is the squadron commander, and now our house is the target of the roof stomp. Due to me being pregnant with twins, the squadron showed us grace by not rudely awakening us, but gave us a few hours of notice to find some sort of refreshments for our festive pilots and spouses.

When the squadron of hungry (and beer-thirsty) pilots ascended on our steps, we were ready with easy but satisfying snacks and plenty of beer, which is what they really wanted in the first place.

LIFE HACK

Have a full beverage refrigerator (of all sorts of delights) and easy snacks. Don't worry if you don't have the perfect food ... eggtopia was born out of desperation and creativity ... but be sure to have the beer.

—*Jenn Steffens*

CEREMONY SURVIVAL

Promotion Ceremonies and Changes of Command are some of the most common military traditions you will ever encounter. Within the first five years of being married to a military member, you will experience at least one if not both.

If you are attending one as a guest, wear something business casual but not overdressed. Come prepared to have a light snack and not a full meal if there is a reception to follow, which most of the time there will be. Make sure you thank the host and congratulate the service member. This is not a place for a long social hour but it does show that you care about the unit and want to make the best of it!

Now, if you are hosting one of the said events, I usually treat it as a Southern tea party! Relaxed and comfortable for all guests in attendance, but classy with tasty food and beverages. Remember you are supporting your military member and you are a representation of him or her. This doesn't mean you have to be perfect (which wouldn't be possible)—just make sure you use the "fine" Chinet plates and you will hit it out of the park!

Lastly, don't presume your children are welcome to these events unless it is stated in the invitation. If in doubt, ask. If they do come, make sure your children know that it is a special time for someone, but realize they might make noise and be prepared with something to entertain them quietly.

The more they attend and are a part of your spouse's events and career, the more they are going to understand the struggles that come with the lifestyle as well.

—*Whitney Messer*

SAY YES TO EVERYTHING

Military traditions create a bond and build morale among service members. Participate in every tradition you can! Also, take the time to understand where it originated and the effects it has on the unit.

I'm currently a military spouse, but I'm also a prior enlisted service member, and I've noticed that either way you serve, there are always odd traditions you'll encounter. The military has countless traditions like pin-on ceremonies, retreat, and my favorite: a combat Dining In/Out, which is a formal dinner with special ceremonies, toasts, and sometimes speeches, dancing, and other frivolities—Dining In is service members only, Dining Out includes a plus one.

During a combat dining in/out, our squadron was able to let loose and enjoy fun and sometimes reckless activities. This one event would bring us all closer together and give us lasting memories that we all still reflect on. In the end, the bigger and messier, the better.

When these events welcome spouses, join! You will not only have a good time, but you will also meet others in a relaxed environment and create a lasting bond with them. You may need to wash chocolate syrup out of your hair afterward, but watching Sgt. Smith go through the gauntlet twice or witnessing when Airman Snuffy stole and wore the Commander's armor will make it all worth it.

Get as involved as possible and even help strategize items to bring. Being part of these weird traditions will not only help build your bond with your spouse but will also allow you to feel more a part of your squadron.

—*Karissa Sylvester*

LIFE HACK

Soggy bread rolls make for great ammo.

WAIT UNTIL YOU'RE ASKED!

Words of wisdom for the newcomer—do not offer advice unless you are specifically asked, no matter how humble you are.

As an officer's wife, I never wore my husband's rank. Ever. Why? Because wives do not wear, or earn, rank. It's just that simple. I realize some wives may intimate or even pretend that they somehow have power by default due to the rank that their husband has, but any feistiness or "power" I had came entirely from the strong Italian woman who raised me.

The following incident has to do with the fact that my husband was an Army officer. I was aware that some did perceive that an officer's wife could wield "power" and I usually was very careful not to do this.

In this instance, three things were involved: I was young, homesick, and thought because I was in my element, I could let my hair down.

I was wrong.

As a child of a divorced secretary, who in turn was raised by my single-parent grandmother, a waitress, I came from humble beginnings. My mother left her job as a secretary and worked for a printer who allowed her to use the front of the store to open up what was to be upstate New York's first thrift shop that was not like those run by the Salvation Army/Goodwill. She called it "The Repitique Shop," and her timing was perfect. The Jimmy Carter Presidency led us to long gas lines and suddenly an upscale secondhand store was a hit.

This is where I worked, in my mother's store, after school and on the weekends almost as soon as I could walk. I was, if you will, a Secondhand Rose. It was in my blood. I learned it from the inside out.

So it was with this attitude and enthusiasm I volunteered at the Thrift Shop for the first time shortly after arriving in Würzburg, Germany. When I walked in, I didn't for a moment think, *I am an officer's wife*—the only officer's wife volunteering that day. I was so excited to be there, it felt like going home.

They were having a Big Bag sale, and I was making my way around the entire store, so thrilled to check out everything and trying to get a feel for the place, when I noticed the bag room and directions on how to fill a bag for their sale. I don't recall exactly what it was, but I do know it was a minor, simple thing, but Mom did something a little better when it came to her Big Bag sale.

I returned to the consignment room/office and mentioned the Bag sale. I then also mentioned that my mom had a thrift store and she did a Big Bag sale in such-and-such a way, and maybe they should consider doing it that way because it was a great success for her as she had a hugely successful thrift store in the Tri-State area of New York that made the *Albany Times Union* and enabled my mother to retire to Florida and buy herself two condos.

I didn't notice anything amiss and finished out my day thinking I was going to love this volunteering thing!

Oh, but there was something very amiss, indeed.

Someone called the next day, and they made it clear the thrift shop ladies were deeply upset that I "threw my husband's rank around" as if I owned the place. The very idea that I tried to change things as if I was the new manager was the final straw.

Stunned, I think I sputtered and tried to defend myself but that ship had sailed.

I was told not to come back again.

In all my years as a volunteer in the military, I had never before, or after, been asked not to volunteer again. It just doesn't happen. That is how much I offended everyone that day.

LIFE HACK

When new, do not offer an opinion. Wait until you are known to the group. Or more importantly, wait until you are asked. *If* you are asked, be prepared for the person or persons asking not to like your frank answer one little bit.

I never should have offered my opinion. I was new, they didn't know me. Like it or not, even though I never wore my husband's rank, they took it that way because I opened my mouth to offer constructive criticism. I didn't say it critically, or so I thought. As I was a stranger, they hadn't asked my opinion, and especially on the first day, I should have kept it to myself no matter how well intentioned. No less as the only officer's wife, I really, *really* should have kept my mouth closed unless it was to make small talk or ask about the families.

I was just a volunteer. I wasn't in a leadership position and regardless, it was not my place.

—*Carol Van Drie*

MILITARY BALLS

Not just a party, but an interview for you! I recommend to forget wearing the sexy dress, just go for the comfortable one. It's never a dull moment when that one spouse or date walks into the ball having opted for the sexy way—all fun and games until a boob pops out!

On a serious note, this is a tradition that is truly fun and exciting. A time where your military member gets to let loose with everyone from lower enlisteds to generals. It is not about you, it's about them! Support them the best way you can by reading up on what happens during a ball from the toast to the speeches. Volunteer to help decorate or be a part of the planning process if you can. Ultimately, let your military member be the star of your show, they truly earned it!

—*Whitney Messer*

YOUR NEW LIFE

Are you military, or are you civilian? As a spouse you are 100 percent in your military counterpart's corner. From day one, until the day they retire, you will live and breathe the military and everything associated with it. You will know your spouse's SSN and birthday better than your own, even after you have kids. Once you add more to the mix, everything still revolves around the spouse no matter what else is going on.

So, why do military spouses occasionally have a hard time fitting in? Well, we need our own lives too, and since we do not report to a command, it can be difficult to find that balance between "I am a part of the military because my spouse is in the military" and "I am a civilian who still has a choice when it comes to certain things."

Every career for every service member is different—some families never move and some move often. We are going on ten years of active duty service and we have moved twelve times (with only two of those being by choice)! Let me tell you, I *hate* moving! But that's a story for another day.

When you decide to take the leap into the full-time military lifestyle, the one thing I can highly recommend is *do not lose yourself*! At least not completely. Sacrifices will be made, more by the spouse rather than the service member. You may have to leave an amazing job or not be able to finish school, or put your dreams on hold. This may only be temporary, or it could be permanent until retirement day.

Whatever happens, just remember dreams and timelines will change and that's okay. My dream has been on hold for a while now and I have finally accepted that. After many moves, four kids, and long hours of work for the service member, my time was better spent taking care of those I loved the most during those times. Do not give up.

Remember that time will come back, and military life is not forever.

—*Whitney Messer*

A Moment

I sit in front of my fireplace,
A sweet flute and heavenly harp play on the satellite radio.
The sun is out this Sunday morning,
I just finished loading more wood for another chilly April day.

The music and solitude make me dream how sweet life is,
And what a serene, special, safe spot it is here.
But then I look upon the fireplace mantle.
An old print of a civil war battle,
Guns a blazing, horses charging, soldiers falling.
On this very ground, in my great granddaddy's time.

It makes me think of my own Dad,
He would find this moment sweet and as life should be.
Often, I would see him grow quiet at times like this.
He would go to some far place, inward.
He would find this moment as how life should be,
But not as life always was.

Those quiet moments I suspect were the horrors he
    remembers,
The beaches of Normandy, the slaughter of the Bulge.
He would never speak of this pain, that would make it too real.
Instead we heard the stories of a wonderful Belgian farm family,
Who fed and protected him, hidden in the cellars of an old
    stone barn,
Full of apples and brandy.

LIFE HACK

Live for the dreams, cherish the moments. Remember the
dark side, but ever so gently.

Life is a paradox!
Sweet, blissful, yet angry and hateful.
Rolling green fields, wildflowers, quiet warm breezes.
Concrete and steel prison cells, the smell of infected bodies,
Tears, rage, regrets . . . and laughter, romance.

My dad was right, live for the dreams, cherish the moments,
Remember the dark side, but ever so quietly.
The old print on the mantle, does it belong there?
Perhaps in a small corner in a darkened room?

A solo violin now plays from the radio,
So sad, so beautiful.

—*Bob Enerson*

PART 3

The Life-Changing Magic of PCSing

THE SEASON OF OPPORTUNITY

PCS (moving) season is always a stressful time. We start thinking of the mile-long to-do list, and everything becomes so daunting and overwhelming. You begin to feel like belongings will never get cleaned up, packed away, or tossed. Not to mention the emotional side of moving. If you're like me, you attach memories to places, and sometimes it can be hard to let go. Maybe your baby took their first steps in your current home. Or you had the best weekly dinners with your duty station friends. I learned that just as everything else, PCSing is part of the life we married. It's a bittersweet time, but it can also be an opportunity for growth.

With a little change of perspective, PCS season can be a great time of reflection to let go of physical and emotional baggage. Let's start with the physical. Moving is stressful for anyone. I watched my parents willingly and excitedly move from their home of eighteen years to a new home of their choice. They were delighted about buying a new house, but the move was very physically draining on them by the end. They never want to do it again! My mom and dad said they never realized how much stuff they owned, until moving it box by box.

We, military families, relocate every few years packing and unpacking our things, time and time again. Moving presents us with the opportunity to sift through our physical baggage several times more than the average family. I always feel so refreshed after sifting through everything! It truly helps make the next duty station feel like a fresh start knowing that we utilize the belongings we have, rather than lugging around boxes for the sake of it!

PCS season is also an emotional time. When we received orders to leave our first duty station, we were devastated. We didn't want to move away from our friends. They became the family we didn't know we needed in such a short amount of time! We had grown attached and comfortable to our life there, but the military always finds a way to shake things up.

We are still very close to those friends—though we're no longer at the same duty station, if it's important enough, you find a way to make long-distance friendships work! As cliché as it is, all good things do come to an end. Having these feelings, whether with a job, spouse's club, mommy's group, church family, or friends, reinforces that your time at your duty station didn't go to waste. Some of those friends or colleagues may remain in your life for years to come.

Always find something positive to cling to with PCSing. It is still my saving grace. I try to think about the fresh start instead of the sadness left behind. You may be excited for a change in jobs, finding places to explore outdoors, clubs or activities offered at the new base, or just a change of scenery. Remember that being uncomfortable usually leads to better opportunities, and that peace can be found with a fresh start. It is always a huge sigh of relief once you see the empty moving truck pull away and know that you are on the other side of a PCS.

LIFE HACK

Always look on the bright side (with less stuff)!

—*Stephanie Dobson*

COLORED TAPE

Every PCS comes with a certain amount of purging of things. Whether it's clothing that no longer fits or has gone out of style to the extra set of pans you picked up somewhere along the line, there are always things that need to go. Designating what needs to *go away* versus what needs to *go* on to your next duty station can be confusing for you, let alone movers or any friends that may be trying to help. If you are moving overseas, you may also have things that need to *go* into long-term storage, just to add more confusion into the mix!

It never seems to fail that movers for UAB, HHG (HHE), and LTS all seem to show up on the same day, or at least in rapid succession. Communicating which of your things are to "go UAB," "go HHG," or "go LTS" is daunting. This is where colored tape can come in handy!

On one of our overseas moves, we had items we were getting rid of, items that were to go to our next home quickly (UAB), items that were to go to our new home (HHG/HHE), items that were to go into storage (LTS), and items we were putting into personal storage for our eldest child who would graduate college before we returned and would probably want her things shortly after graduation.

Using different colored tape on our things and a neatly handwritten key with each tape color in each room, we were able to quickly and easily communicate which items were to go where. In our case, blue went to personal storage, zebra stripe for HHG (HHE), yellow indicated UAB, and green for LTS. No tape meant ask us or do not touch. Tape was placed on corners of furniture or used to designate entire sections of rooms. Nothing replaces an eagle-eye on the movers, but colored tape definitely helped us, the movers, and the friends that popped up to help.

—*Diana Ringquist*

"THREE MOVES IS AS GOOD AS A FIRE"
—BARBARA STANSBERRY*

Marie Kondo's message in her bestselling book, *The Life Changing Magic of Tidying Up*, of letting go of things which no longer serve a purpose has nothing on the military or foreign service move schedule. Being forced to review everything you own every few years (or less) and having weight allowances prevents the accumulation of too much *stuff.*

Force yourself to open every box or agree to get rid of it unopened after you have moved it twice without review. Give away the children's clothing that no longer fits and toss out the truly broken and damaged. Find out early in your new assignment where the recycling and thrift shops are located. These community resources can be used throughout your stay, and when it comes time to PCS, you'll know where you can drop off donations. By the time you have moved three times, only those things you truly value will still be with you at your fourth home.

Your "Must Haves"
Starting Day 1, decide what things you absolutely cannot live without. Be realistic. You can live without your favorite snack food and your favorite shampoo, you just may not want to do so. Prioritize. Create a list that is divided into levels of importance. The top level should include things such as medication for chronic or acute conditions and important records, such as licenses ((driver's, marriage, professional), medical records, birth certificates, Power of Attorney papers, and passports.

The next level should include items that you can probably replace, but it may take time or be costly. These can be your computer, televisions, a special stuffed animal, or sporting equipment, depending on your family's interests. These items should be used regularly. If you only lift weights or watch a TV once a month or less, you should lower the priority.

---

*Barbara Stansberry (1935–2019) was a registered nurse, teacher, and school board president, as well as a mother, friend, and hero.

Third level are things that you love. If you are moving overseas, this can be a tricky set of decisions based on where you are going. Some posts may be susceptible to ordered departures and those beloved things may be left behind.

Continue down your priority list with five groups at most. The last group or two can be left behind, given away, or put into storage.

—*Diana Ringquist*

NEIGHBORS

I don't know how many different homes you have lived in, but for me, it's been a lot. Twenty-two different homes in my short and very youthful thirty-five years of life.

First, I have to admit that without realizing it, I picked up a lot of ways on how to be a good neighbor from my amazing mother! Being a military brat my entire childhood, and then marrying a man in the army, I only knew life where you moved every year or two, and therefore get a whole new set of neighbors that often.

Well, while I was growing up, my mom would always be the first to bring food over, offer help, invite neighbors over for dinner, or offer to babysit their kids, and I could go on with how giving she was. Now, almost instinctively when I would become someone's neighbor (or even roommate), I would do the same, and realized really quickly that a little generosity and kindness can go a long way.

Remember, your neighbors will probably see or hear you at your weakest points, and your highest points. Your ugliest of times, and the prettiest of times. Make an effort to get to know them, and be kind and generous, and your brief stay at your new duty station could turn around from being super lonely, to a block party every night.

—*Allison Wood*

LABEL *EVERYTHING* BEFORE THE MOVERS COME

At one point when the children were little and I was operating on sleep-deprivation mode (read: comatose), we PCSed from one end of the country to the other. The movers arrived to pack our house into boxes, and on our walk-through, I vaguely pointed toward the various rooms and noted the giant pile of baby and toddler "essentials" that shouldn't get boxed up (those essentials traveled cross-country with us on top of the car, along with two kids and two cats, but that drive is another story).

So, without further direction from me, they boxed up everything else. I mean *everything* else. When we started unpacking boxes in our new home, we found a box filled with *an entire shelf's worth of spare hardware* from our old house—a rental. Our old landlord was extremely gracious about the mistake, but it taught me to label everything with sticky notes. "Pack" and "Don't pack." Also, take your time with the walk-through with the packers when they arrive. Point out your helpful sticky notes (remember to feed the packers and buy them water, too).

By the way, when we arrived in our new house and were unpacking all our boxes, we found an empty Coke can—all wrapped up in packing paper—in the spare hardware box. Because of course that must clearly have appeared to be a necessity for when we arrived in our new home. Decoration, perhaps?

—*Heather Murphy Capps*

ROOM STAGING

Some moves allow you to prepack. Other moves will find your packers unpacking your things in order to repack them. Ask at your pre-move inspection. Any way you look at it, you will need to divide and conquer your possessions.

Prepare your rooms by "staging" them. Sort what you can into groupings or piles that will be going together. Put all your UAB items together in one room. All your HHG (HHE) items to the left in each room, and your giveaways to the right. You can use tape (see "Colored Tape" on page 26) to divide areas as well. Everything behind this tape, like in a crime scene, is not to be packed. Regardless of how you prepare your rooms, be sure you have plenty of signs to reinforce your different categories. If overseas, you may need to add the local language.

Finally, have a space for your movers. This can be as simple as a corner in a room that you stock with water bottles and/or snacks. It is always a good idea to provide at least water and/or cups for your movers. Remaining hydrated is essential for them to do their job and focus on ensuring your belongings are properly packed. Even if they choose not to accept your offerings, the gesture goes a long way.

Also have a basket or shoebox for them as a safe place to put the truck keys and anything else they want to keep safe from accidental packing. I have seen more than one moving vehicle early the next morning with a note in the window pleading not to tow the truck as they accidentally packed their keys and had to drive back to the main office for the spares.

—*Diana Ringquist*

SOME DIFFERENT IDEAS FOR PACKING DAY

Our first army PCS was a unicorn. Nothing damaged, nothing lost or stolen. The second PCS, much was stolen. After that move I kept a document of *every* single item we owned and the quantity.

Now, after fifteen years of PCSing, my speech to the movers is this: "The only thing my husband cares about are the two TVs; I care about everything else. But we have had so many items stolen from us (we've replaced three PlayStations), that if you want *anything* in my house, please ask me and I will probably give it to you."

The movers look at me in disbelief every time I give this speech—I tell them I am serious. The last set of movers took me up on it; she saw an extra PS3 and asked if she could have it. We said yes, and gave her that and all the games that went with it. Nothing from that move was damaged or lost.

Since my husband only cares about the TVs (and we have two 65-inch sets, because who doesn't need two?!), I go out the morning before the movers come and get a newspaper. I take a photo with the date of the newspaper clearly visible and in front of the TV to show that there is no damage to the screens.

Pack out days I look at as days to hang out one last time with my girlfriends. I usually bring over Starbucks and some yummy goodies and we sit and chat and watch over the packers. Nothing scarier to packers than a bunch of seasoned military wives watching them pack.

—*Diana Ringquist*

THE WORST PART IS OVER

The worst part of the PCS is the lead up to it, kind of like an unaccompanied tour or deployment. You know it's coming, you dread it every day and then the day comes, and you tear the band-aid off.

No matter what—you will get through it. It will happen whether you want it to or not. You will lose things, you will break things, you will have to spend tons of unnecessary money to buy new things . . . but it will be okay. Two months after your PCS when you are all settled, pictures are hung, and kids are in their new school, it will be like it never happened. Until the next time you have to PCS . . .

> ## LIFE HACK
>
> Treat your movers with respect. Feed them, tip them, but watch them like a hawk.

—*Yvette Hulsman*

Hacks: 1) Do what you love. 2) Say hello. 3) Volunteer where appropriate. 4) Invite and host.

Here you are again. Another new place, new (to you) house, new neighborhood, new area to explore, new state, new weather, and new friends to make . . . feels like you're starting from scratch.

While the thought of new beginnings might seem shiny to most (and maybe if you're lucky, to you too most times), to some of us it can feel like another arduous journey to get back to our comfort zone. And while your close friends are only a phone call away, chances are there are none in the general vicinity. Thankfully I've been in this situation so many times in my life I've developed a few methods I'll share to help break the ice and get you to meet some new friends fast.

I moved around most of my life as a military brat and then again numerous times as an adult because of . . . well, life. I was always the new girl. I've even had a job doing business development where I attended numerous networking events, breakfasts, lunches, dinners, galas, and industry seminars where I knew no one and had to make and develop relationships. That all-too-familiar feeling of not knowing anybody followed me around my whole life.

My husband jokes that when he bought his first townhouse and lived there for five years, he knew no one, but just a month after I moved in, we knew the whole neighborhood. How did that happen? No worries, I'll tell you.

Hack #1: Do what you love. I know this sounds cheesy, but think about your regular routine. What do you like to do most days? What do you like to do for fun? Hobbies or exercise routines are a great place to start. I currently have a two-year-old at home so I try to get out and walk every day.

I can't tell you how many people I've met walking. You will naturally find people with similar interests doing the same things that interest you. As there will always be people out doing these similar interests, this is where the next hack comes into play.

Hack #2: Say hello! Break the silence and introduce yourself. It seems so obvious but a lot of us tend to avoid this step. You either get lost in your phone or feel like you're forcing a conversation so you limit yourself to the noncommittal head nod or a half smile.

I say hi to most people I come into contact with whether I'm getting something out of my car and see a neighbor drive by or I'm out walking with my son and see another mom. Say hello, introduce yourself, ask them to join you on walks, let them know you're new in town...chances are you'll see them again.

Hack #3: One of the best ways to meet people is to volunteer. From professional to lifestyle organizations, there are countless means. You've just moved to a new school district—can you volunteer with the school? Get involved with the classroom, the PTA, you'll meet tons of other parents and parents of your kid's classmates. The same goes for professional organizations, volunteering is a great way to network and give back. I volunteered to develop a mentorship program for a professional organization and came away with not only knowledge of program development but also the pleasure of getting to know fifty new peers and seasoned professionals.

Now the final hack is how you turn an acquaintance into a possible friend. It's probably the most important hack and what I've found to be the most successful tool in my social arsenal.

Hack #4: Invite and host. Whatever the commonality, if you met them out walking, invite them to walk or hike. You could start your own walking club. If you met them out at a winery invite them to a happy hour or wine night at your house. This is applicable to any interest—cooking, drinking, art, play dates, sports, exercise, or other hobbies.

I host a ton of events, anything from morning coffee or afternoon tea, to play dates and lunch, dinners, cookbook club, ladies' nights in, bourbon and whiskey tastings, poker nights, or neighborhood-wide happy hours. I don't wait around to be invited. If I want to see someone, I reach out to them. Don't wait, just start. Start with something easy like coffee. You can do it.

There is a nursery rhyme song that my son is currently listening to and it holds true and dear to my heart:

The more we get together
Together, together
The more we get together
The happier we'll be
'Cause your friends are my friends
And my friends are your friends

—*Olivia Devescovi*

PCS

Those three letters will cause you to have a Love/Hate relationship with that part of the military. It will either be the worst move or the best move. There will be nothing in between. The one hack I can recommend is *downsize* whatever you can and only keep the sentimental items. If you need to buy a certain item when you get to your new home, that's okay!

There will always be a military family moving when you get to your next duty station that is selling something they don't need. I have decided that when retirement comes, I am going to start my own packing business but will make sure packing the full trash can is not on that list! Yes, this can really happen, as it isn't up to the movers to determine what is trash and what isn't. Make sure to empty and wash out all trash cans. Never a fun box to open when you haven't seen it in over two weeks!

—*Whitney Messer*

YOUR "NO-GO" ROOM

When preparing for your movers to arrive, start with designating one room as the "No-Go" room. This is a room where the movers are not allowed under any circumstances. Choose this room with some thought based on your needs and situation. Generally, I choose a bathroom. Having one bathroom as a "No-Go" space means you likely have a lock on the door and you will have a place that only you and your family can use. If your "No-Go" room does not have a lock, put a sign on the door ("Vicious Animal Inside" tends to work) and use tape across the door like they do in television crime shows.

A "No-Go" room is a place to keep your items safe from accidental packing and it also provides you with a space away from the chaos of the pack where you can hide out for a few minutes to catch your breath if you need. Your "No-Go" room could contain any of the following:

Pets
Pet food
Luggage
Jewelry
Giveaway items
House keys
Car keys
Important documents and medical records
Beloved toys
Any items you borrowed and must return (library books, small
    appliances, neighbor's plates, etc.)
Anything else you do not want the movers to accidentally
    pack

—*Diana Ringquist*

PCS PREP: THE PURGE

As soon as you have an RFO (Request for Orders, or preliminary orders) in hand, it's time to engage in a time-honored pre-move tradition known as *The Purge*. This requires a certain ruthlessness and single-minded focus that can only be gained from the experience of prior PCS moves. It's a mindset one enters into that simply relies on this one determining question: "Do I really want to move this again?"

"This" could be any number of things, depending on your current stage of life. It may be the baby swing that has been disassembled and reassembled through so many moves that there is no way it's still a safe place for an infant. As Elsa would say, "Let it go!"

It may be a dresser that is currently held together with duct tape and Gorilla Glue. Have a moment of honesty with yourself and admit it will not survive the manhandling of movers or even a slight accidental bump of a laundry basket as you walk by. Give it the old "thank you for your service" and send it on its way.

The box of books your spouse adamantly assures you he/she needs *just in case* but has actually never been opened or unpacked even once during the last four moves? Goodbye. At this point, there's probably a family of mice living in there anyway. Don't even open it. Just quietly and reverently place it in the donation pile.

Don't ask your spouse for permission to do this. If one day he or she asks you "Hey, where is that box of calculus and geography textbooks from 2004?" (spoiler alert: they will never ask you this), just casually but firmly blame it on the movers . . . "it was lost/damaged/mislabeled/fell of the truck . . ." whatever, it's your choice as any of these scenarios has happened or will happen.

The point is, let's not be moving things we aren't using or haven't unpacked from the last move. Purge with purpose! Purge without sentiment! Purge while your spouse and kids are not at home! Play the long game and remove one or two items of said boxes every Purge cycle. Eventually those boxes will be empty. Work smarter, not harder.

—*Katie Landis*

PREPARE FOR MOVERS BY ORGANIZING AHEAD OF TIME

The Container Store is your New Happy Place. One year (the actual year/country/current mental state elude me), I was psyching myself up for a bit of unpacking after a PCS overseas. I told myself that after ten minutes of non-distracted work, then I would treat myself to some coffee. I grabbed one of the small kitchen knives or scissors that were hazardously littered about the apartment from my routine of cutting a box open, putting the knife down, immediately losing it, then getting another one out of the drawer.

I cut open a medium-sized box marked "master bath." Inside were some bath items, clothes from my closet, some cuter clothes from my daughter's closet, and . . . a toaster. I may be a little unorthodox, but keeping a toaster in the bathroom is not a habit of mine.

This happens because professional movers must pack heavy items along with some light ones in order to manage the weight of each box. But with frequent moves, it gets old to have your household goods randomly thrown together. On some of our moves, a few boxes remained unopened, such as ones marked "garage," when we moved from a house to an apartment. You may end up replacing an item simply because you couldn't find it and lost the will to keep looking.

I have come up with a system that helps me know roughly what is in each box before I open it. Prior to the movers arriving, I place things to be packed together in the same room. For example, all bathroom items from the whole house are placed in one bathroom. All the linens in one room, etc. Unbreakable items I want to keep organized in one box, like sweaters, I use clear, waterproof containers so I can see what's inside, then tape up the container, or else the movers will "helpfully" open and repack, then throw in a coffee maker for good measure.

Also, I leave a sticky note: "Do not open" or "Pack as is." They usually ask me to sign that it has been packed by the owner. If the items cannot be damaged, it's worth it. At the new home, no unpacking necessary. I can put away three boxes in no time and get to my coffee before it's cold.

—*Kristen Riffle*

THE ONE THING NOT TO ASK FOR

We'll let you in on a little secret, which every experienced military spouse knows, but is never, ever mentioned.

We tend to be a tight group, helping each other through thick and thin. The good times are very, very good, and the bad . . . well, let's not go there. But there is almost always someone close by to share a glass of wine, an empty seat in a carpool, or a shoulder to cry on. Meals will magically appear in times of need, a sack of lightly used clothes for your rapidly growing toddler can be had with a few clicks in a Facebook group.

But the one thing you can never ask for, or expect, is help unpacking your household goods. It's an unwritten rule. Don't be surprised if your new neighbors show up with a six-pack of beer, and perch on a box while you continue to unwrap everything you weren't looking for. But the task is yours alone. Once you've done it a couple or twenty times, you'll understand why.

—*Tracey Enerson Wood*

PRE-PACKING FOR MOVES: SWEAT THE SMALL STUFF

As a young, recently married military wife, I remember hearing those sweet words, "you know, the military sends people to pack everything *for you* every time you move."

What this message fails to emphasize is what *everything* really means. That paper clip you couldn't live without in your junk drawer? Lovingly wrapped in three pieces of packing paper. The four pages left on the almost-finished post-it note pad? Wrapped and taped like a Christmas package.

We do not always have time to go through our junk drawers before we move. What I have learned through more than five moves (I can't keep count, can you?), I do have time to dump my junk drawer into a gallon-size zip-top bag, then I put that bag back in the drawer. Then when the packers pack the contents of that drawer, I don't open lots of rolled-up paper filled with bits and pieces of junk. That way that paper clip I can't live without makes the move with the rest of his friends.

This works for baby sock drawers or any kind of drawer, really. Just get bigger bags accordingly.

LIFE HACK

Pack that junk drawer in gallon-size bags before the movers get to it.

—*Lauren Walsh and Carol Van Drie*

BLANKIES, BINKIES, AND BINS

As an Army Infantry wife for thirty-two years, I consider twenty-one moves in those years almost all-consuming. Of course, it wasn't the only way I contributed to my husband's time in the Army, but it certainly made up a lion's share of the time. Preparing for the move, executing the move, surviving the move, getting to our new duty station, settling in, and beginning our new life in our new home seemed as much a part of being an army wife as anything else I did.

Perhaps that's the reason I tend to think of ways to make those moves easier.

One tip is, whenever possible, double or even triple up on anything that is near and dear. If your two-year-old has a special blankie, make certain you bring an identical one with you on that move. Do not trust that blankie to the movers or even stuffed "somewhere" in an extra bin or box you bring along.

Like the extra set of car keys you bring with you on that cross-country drive to the next base, you have that blankie at the ready because if, God forbid, your little one loses *the* very blankie they cannot possibly fall asleep without somewhere between Salt Lake City, Utah, and Valparaiso, Indiana, you will be thrilled with yourself when you can whip the extra one you have stashed away and say, "No, Honey, it's right here!" just before bedtime that night.

Keep it with the extra binkies, and if you can possibly make room, stash more than one.

—*Carol Van Drie*

WHEN TO LET GO

For me, a type-A control freak, becoming part of an organization where you have little to no control over many facets of your life was a steep learning curve. Not only was there a huge nameless and faceless organization telling us where we had to live and when we had to move, but during our PCS, I had to get all the related information relayed through my husband. He was also trying to juggle his primary job along with managing our PCS. I would drive us both crazy!

The biggest takeaway for me over sixteen years, eight PCSs, and eleven total moves, was to learn what I had control over and manage those processes to the best of my ability and let the rest go. In the beginning I would get spun up and stressed out. I would lose sleep and be a ball of anxiety but not actually accomplish much.

Over the years my husband would hand over PCS-related tasks to me, which I loved because it gave me an outlet for my energy and satisfied my need to feel like I had at least a little control in what can feel like a very unnerving process.

During our last PCS from one embassy posting to another, we were about a month from "wheels up" with no orders and therefore no ability to pack out, buy airline tickets, or even confirm on what date we could depart.

We were required to take leave in between our assignments so we were essentially planning a vacation to visit family in two different states along with managing our PCS. Our personal leave required the purchase of additional airline tickets and hotel reservations; none of which could be booked until we knew we could depart our post on our projected date.

Old me: *Freaking out.* Me now: *What can I do to move this along?*

My husband travels frequently for his job, so he did not have the time or ability to chase down his orders. I took on this task and reached out to the office which initiates orders. I was able to finally speak to his assigned Airman who required specific documents to be sent again. Since my husband copied me on all previous communications,

I had the files saved so I could easily forward them and was able to keep the process moving forward.

All this to say, try to work as a team with your spouse, take one step at a time, and learn what is worth stressing over and what is simply a waste of your time and energy.

—*Jessica Lindville*

RECEIVED ORDERS, NOW WHAT?

Once you have orders, I'm sure *Here we go again* crosses your mind. However, nowadays it's much easier to get acclimated to your new duty station before you show up, even weeks before you do!

First, start telling everyone you know where you are going. In the military community, someone will know someone who is probably at your next duty session. Also, check your social media accounts to see if maybe an acquaintance of yours is stationed there—you might already have a built-in network!

Lastly, don't be shy, join Facebook pages for that Base/Post and don't be scared to ask questions in those groups either. That is what they were designed for!

—*Lesley Gagnon*

PART 4

Getting Accustomed to Having No Money

A LITTLE SALT WATER AND A LIFETIME MEMORY

My parents always struggled financially, with six kids to clothe, feed, and keep a roof over their heads. So I grew up knowing how to squeeze the last cent out of a dime. My mom could "make Lincoln cry." Those skills came in handy when I was a newlywed army wife.

Many years ago, when we were stationed in Ft. Benning, Georgia, I would make the six-hour drive to Jacksonville to see my parents as often as I was able. After returning from one such trip, my dad called me and said, "You forgot your contact lens stuff. Do you want me to send it to you?"

I thought I had left a sleeve of the little enzyme tablets, which would be easy to stick in an envelope. He didn't write often, but when he did, he wrote the sweetest, most loving letters, so I selfishly said, "Sure. That stuff can be pretty expensive."

About a week later, I got a package from him in the mail, a little smaller than a shoe box. I opened it to find several wads of crumbled newspaper, and then, carefully wrapped like a fragile crystal ornament, was a small pink bottle of contact lens solution. The cheap stuff—just preserved salt water for rinsing. It had maybe half an ounce left in it.

We lost him shortly after that, and since then, I've probably cried more tears than was salt water in that bottle, thinking of my dad taking such time and care, just because I told him I needed it. At the time, I thought it was such a waste of time and money to send it, although I would never tell him that. He did include a short letter, which of course was the much more precious thing.

I still think of it to this day, and he's been gone nearly thirty years. Maybe it wasn't such a waste, after all.

LIFE HACK

Be careful what you ask for from loved ones.
And see the love in the little things.

—*Tracey Enerson Wood*

BABYSITTERS

Moving to a new place is difficult on so many levels. Thankfully, we all get settled in eventually! Next step is making friends, exploring the post/base, and adventuring out around the local town—however, in order to do so, you'll need to find a reliable babysitter!

Well, I found the most comforting, easiest, and cheapest way to do this was to swap babysitting duty with a neighbor or friend! It can be awkward at first but put yourself out there and start asking around if any couple would be willing to watch your kids for three hours one night and you watch their kids for three hours another night.

Also, if you find someone open to it, but they have four kids, and you have one (or vice versa), ask that you watch their kids once they go to sleep so the task isn't quite so lopsided. Or if you're the one with four kids, offer the same, or pay your friend in gift cards to their favorite restaurant, or even clean up their whole house!

In the long run, having some nights away with your spouse at your new duty station, with the help of a trusted neighbor or friend is well worth it.

—Allison Wood

INSURANCE FOR EVERYTHING

Check your insurance coverage before and after every move. Your location, the location of your possessions, and your family structure will change. Take the time to be sure that you are fully covered. Ensure copies of those documents are available to you (printed or electronic) at all times and be certain you have the contact information for both the person that sold you the policy and the claims department in case you need help down the road.

Don't forget your long-term storage, pets before, during, and after travel, and even beloved things that you leave in the care of family or friends. Why? Because tornadoes can happen in New Jersey even if you are in N'Djamena.

—Diana Ringquist

WHEN IN DOUBT, BRING A SPARE AND DON'T FORGET THE EXTRA UNIFORM BITS

It's important to keep in mind those little things that may slip your service member's mind. Make sure there are extra buttons, backings, patches, ranks, and whatnot for the uniform. They will get lost, broken, otherwise disappear, or maybe new is needed.

Similarly, extra sewing supplies in the form of small kits purchased or made can be the answer to a myriad of surprises that come with moves. Apply this rule to all areas of your family—an extra CAC reader, an extra toy, extra school supplies, extra collar/leash for your pet, or an extra copy of some of your important documents. To keep documents from getting lost in transit, carry them yourself.

If you are still worried, send a duplicate set to a trusted family member or friend who is not likely to move and is willing to hang on to them for you.

—*Diana Ringquist*

DOUBLE MEALS, HALF THE WORK

A lot of us starting out in the military certainly do not make a lot of money. When you don't have much money it can be very hard to plan meals for picky eaters. It can get old going through the same recipes every month, and the stress of finding, choosing, and cooking new meals can be huge especially when you aren't sure anyone in your family will even like it! Time and money are too precious!

One way to hack your way out of situations like this (or if you're looking for a way to spice up your meal plan routine) is to start asking other spouses what meals they make. Then when you find someone who makes similar categories of meals you make, ask if they would double their recipe one day a week and give you the leftovers for that night, and then you would do the same with a meal you make the same week. You could switch meals once a week!

This solves not having to cook one night a week, not having to eat leftovers, and not being as wasteful because buying in bulk is usually cheaper.

—*Lesley Gagnon*

SAVING FOR PCS

The military does pay for the major PCS expenses (travel, transport, and packing of home goods, food, etc.), but you need to be prepared for the miscellaneous expenses and each move has its unique expenses.

First, as a working spouse I find myself without our second income for at least seven months during the transition period—that's a lot of money. I have also noticed that during this transition period we end up transferring a lot of money from savings to handle the miscellaneous expenses (around $10,000). Some expenses we find consistent every place we move are the following:

- Pet fee for new rental between $150–$350.
- Two months' rent to sign a new lease.
- Transfer and administrative fees for each utility account . . . fifteen dollars here and twenty dollars there.
- Never-ending Walmart runs for products and supplies that could not be included in the home goods shipment.
- Car repairs for the long-distance moves.
- Will you need to ship your pet? Between $250–$2,000; we got lucky and got to SPACE-A our pet for $250.
- Going OCONUS? Expect to pay a big vet fee for the foreign travel paperwork, updated vaccines, microchipping, shipping crate, and supplies.
- Car inspections at your new duty station.

As soon as we finally get settled in and get that second income back, I immediately start saving up for the next move. It takes the stress off my shoulders when we have money set aside just for the next big PCS. If you know you are going to move every three years, it can't hurt to move a small portion every month into savings whether you have a second income or not, and even if it's just $25 a month, making it a habit is what counts!

—Superwoman

MANAGING THE WEEKNIGHT MEALS

With busy family life, feeding the gang dinner on weeknights is often a stress-filled ordeal. You can waste lots of money on fast food and pre-packaged convenience foods, or you can do a little preparation and save money and eat healthier.

Make a list of all the non-perishable pantry items your family enjoys, and buy them in bulk when they go on sale. Don't go overboard, you need to have room to safely store it all. About six months' worth is plenty.

When planning a meal, it usually rotates around your protein, and this is usually your most expensive grocery item, so try to buy extras when they are on sale. For example, if a store has a special on ground beef, and that's something you cook with, buy enough for three family meals. Boneless chicken thighs are also a good staple for many recipes.

Then, prepare, cook, then drain the fat. Include vegetables you typically like too, for example, onions, bell peppers, and mushrooms work well in lots of dishes. You may want to freeze an extra package of the meat for future recipes. Save a third of the cooked meat and vegetables for that night's meal. Divide the remaining food into two, wrap them each in aluminum foil (optional, helps prevent freezer burn), then place in zip-top bags or sealable plastic containers. Label the bags or the foil with a permanent marker with the date and contents and freeze.

Now, next time you have a super-busy day and need a quick dinner, take out one of your frozen meal starters. The above combination is good for spaghetti sauce, chili, stew, shepherd's pie, sloppy joes, etc. You just change the seasonings, and add sauce or whatever else you need to complete your recipe.

—*Tracey Enerson Wood*

THINGS TO CONSIDER WHEN CHOOSING A RENTAL

I think looking for a new place to live is probably one of the most fun things to do. So many different layouts to consider, neighborhoods, amenities, styles, and colors of homes to choose from.

I'm sure most of you reading this book know exactly what you want and do not want in your house, if it has a two-car garage or a backyard, three or four bedrooms, proximity to the city, but can you see what kind of landlord you're getting just by looking at the house?

You know that saying "You are what you eat"? Well, your house sure says a lot about you whether you realize it or not. I'm going to share with you little hacks we've learned through the process of renting and things to consider during your first walk-through when searching for rentals.

We've moved around quite a bit in our lives. My husband and I are both brats and somehow continued the tradition of moving every year or so well into our thirties. I didn't pick up these nuggets of wisdom until having lived in a couple of houses where our rental search was a foreshadowing of the actual rental experience. These signs are present when you first tour a home and we just weren't used to looking for them.

Money invested in the house is a great indicator for how much your future landlord is going to care about future repairs and maintenance. Pay close attention to the exterior of the home. Is the lawn kept and manicured? Is there a fence or deck? Is it falling apart or rotting? Does the house need a major power wash? Is there siding or roof shingles missing? Are there trees growing from the gutters? Were the garden beds mulched? Are there any forgotten piles of wood/leaves/trash? Are there tons of cracks in the driveway? Are there any huge bare areas in the grass? Is the backyard fenced? Is there a different fence that borders each neighbor?

On the inside of the house, has it been updated? If so, was the quality of the material used to update high-end? Average? Cheap? What type of material is used for the updates? Is it all the least expensive material? What do the appliances look like? Are they forty years old? What style is the refrigerator? Is it something small that doesn't even take up the full allotted space of the refrigerator area? If so, run!

Is there carpet in the house? Is it freshly cleaned but also more than fifteen years old? Does the whole house need a new paint job? When's the last time they re-caulked the shower and tub areas? Do the window treatments look like they need some kind of treatment?

Does the landlord have a maintenance schedule? Beware of "as needed" responses. They should be cleaning gutters at least once a year, sometimes twice (if there are trees near the house), and servicing AC and furnace at least once a year—this also checks for any mold that may be setting up shop in the systems. Make sure the rental agreement doesn't put all the maintenance on you, either. You don't want to be servicing AC, furnaces, gutter cleanings, etc. Be sure to ask how they prep the house between listings. Are the carpets professionally cleaned? If there's a fireplace, when was the last time it was serviced?

Generally speaking, a property management company or professional is a good first sign. Don't get me wrong, some landlords are very good and responsive and take this job seriously to repair things in a speedy manner. Most of us take pride in our homes! It can be helpful if there's a professional buffer for communication between you and the landlord if possible.

Lastly, walk around and ring some doorbells. Talk to your future neighbors. They can tell you what the demographic is of the street, where all the families with kids live, how long they've lived there, if there's any major problems with the homes (flyover zones, prone to flooding, etc.), what they think of the schools.

If you've found a house that is well maintained, then odds are you've found a great rental. Hopefully I've equipped you with some awareness to take on your next walk-through. Happy hunting!

—*Olivia Devescovi*

FUN AND CHEAP WAYS TO MEET NEW PEOPLE

I was a new spouse stationed overseas when I heard there was a coupon-clipping event for spouses. I thought this would be a great way to meet new people and decided to go. However, when I arrived, I saw only one other person in the room, and my nerves and anxiety overcame me, and I ran out of there!

Afterwards, still determined to meet new people, I created my own coffee outing. After several meet-ups, I realized the key ingredient to make it a success was to make sure you had one other person to attend the event with you. This way, no new arrivals would be faced with only one other person in the room.

Overall, after seventeen years of military spousal-hood, my best advice to meet people on a budget is to start new groups and to join groups, but always bring a friend! Start or join your FRG, Bases' and Posts' Facebook groups in areas of interest, weekly/monthly coffees, book clubs, etc.

—*Lesley Gagnon*

PART 5

Are We There Yet?

PREPARATION IS KEY

Most people have traveled internationally at some point. Even if you haven't, with a little bit of reading and asking you can generally figure out your way through airports and onto planes, navigating check in, security, and even dreaded transfers.

But what about when you are PCSing? What about when you are moving your whole life and family to a place that more than likely doesn't have a direct flight?

I'll set the scene. Two adults, a baby, nine suitcases, one stroller, and one car seat.

Your first challenge is to get to the airport. What taxi is going to fit that load? Once you figure that out, you then have to figure out how to get everything into the airport to check in for your flight. I recommend giving yourself many additional hours to go through this process, even though you may have to wait a while to board, at least you *may* be a little less stressed and somewhat less sweaty by the time you do.

Once you have paid the excess baggage fees (make sure to check with the airlines, many waive fees for military on orders) and made it through security, you can breathe, just a little. You still have multiple hours ahead of you, trapped in a tin can with a wriggly baby.

In our instance we were *lucky* enough to have *only* one transfer—and it was through Frankfurt, a first-world country, and a seemingly less-intimidating airport. They make it sound so simple. Land. Get bags. Go to another terminal. Check in and recheck bags. Go through security. Board your plane and boom, it's that simple! Nope!

No one takes into consideration that "getting your bags" means trying to fit everything onto two luggage carts because that's the maximum number two people can push (while wearing a baby). Then moving those precariously balanced carts to where you need to go. Frankfurt is great in that it has a wonderful tram that will take you from one terminal to the next. What they don't tell you is that you cannot take the luggage carts onto said tram. So now comes the nightmare. Trying to figure out how to get *all of your stuff* to another building.

Here are your options:

- Catch a cab, or in our case, three cabs, because one simply will not fit your luggage.
- Walk. We tried this. It's not easy. It's up hill and on sidewalks that are not made for luggage carts. I do not recommend it, hence hailing three cabs halfway.
- Divide and conquer. This is the route we took on our return voyage, two years and one kid later. We landed, got bags, and still dealt with the Tetris task of balancing and maneuvering the carts. But now, we worked smarter and not harder. With that much luggage we knew we would have to make multiple trips in order to use the tram, which is definitely the most efficient way.
- Unfortunately, you cannot leave bags unattended on either end so you can't simply make those multiple trips back and forth. The trick is to make use of the luggage storage. Yes, it will cost you, but it's worth it. Trust me. My husband and I each loaded ourselves with children and as many bags as we could manage and we checked the rest into the storage facility. We made our way to the next terminal and found a spot to camp. I got comfortable with the kids and guarded the bags that had made this initial trip with us. Hubby went back to get the rest. Sure, we spent some money just to keep our bags safe for a short amount of time but in my opinion, it was money well spent. Again, we were able to check in for our flight a little bit less stressed and way less sweaty.

So this may seem like a simple solution but it's not something you want to be figuring out on the go. Not all airports have storage facilities and if they do, they can be tricky to find. For us it took a terrible experience on the way there for us to find a solution for the way back. There was no way we were repeating that fateful day from two years prior.

—*Victoria Griffith*

RESEARCH YOUR NEXT POST
(BUT DON'T BELIEVE EVERYTHING YOU HEAR)

Congratulations on your next assignment! Jump online and find out everything you can. Ask around if anyone has been there and what they can tell you about it. If you have a sponsor, ask them about the area, activities, family or single life, and your special interests or hobbies. Ask all those things you want to know!

Then ask someone else. Ask another person after that. Get as many different perspectives and opinions as possible, because they are just that—perspectives and opinions. One person's "best post ever" can be the next person's "grounds for divorce."

Not every assignment is completely great nor completely terrible. Manage your expectations on both ends of the spectrum and remember that every post is 90 percent what you make it. Don't aim to survive, aim to thrive and bloom!

—Diana Ringquist

HURRY UP AND WAIT

Are we there yet? That question is usually the most-asked question from my kids when we go anywhere longer than to the Chick-fil-A drive through!

From the adult side, that can be associated with any aspect of the military. Whether it be driving/flying to a new duty station, waiting on orders, or the long twelve-hour shift work schedule that will never come to an end. The saying "hurry up and wait" is a term you will quickly learn. Could be even before your spouse joins the service!

I feel there are times when I ask my husband "why?" And "how long?" more than my kids do. Just accept it! There is so much you won't be able to change. You cannot rush military and their processes. Just get yourself a good book, a hobby, have a kid, or take a drive and sit back and wait. You will get there when you get there!

—Whitney Messer

NEVER BELIEVE WHAT YOU HEAR
(BOOTS ON THE GROUND ... AND KITCHEN SETUP)

The man with the clipboard looked completely exasperated. I stood in my doorway, feet apart, hands on hips, with a determined look on my face.

"We are to move you to your new home today," he repeated as if I hadn't heard him the first five times. "It's right here in the papers," he shook the clipboard for emphasis.

"No," I repeated. "I'm not moving. My kitchen is finally set up. Change your paperwork."

It was at that moment I noticed a neighbor in the distance waving his arms. "Are you sure you're supposed to move Unit 2? Perhaps you're supposed to move Unit 12," I suggested as I nodded my head toward the neighbor.

The man shuffled through his papers again, his expression changing abruptly. "Oh, I'm so sorry! You are correct, it is Unit 12. The one looked like a zero—my apologies."

Not all such faceoffs end in your favor. Orders change or are cancelled. Possessions are sent ahead only to be rerouted at some point after you've been diverted. Rumors can abound and opinions will fly during assignment and PCS seasons. I have had friends at the gate in the airport who have been turned around, or in mid-flight when new orders are issued.

The move next year has been pushed up to next month, the four-month assignment has been extended to two years, and the accompanied tour has changed status and is now unaccompanied. Prepare for your PCS move, but always be prepared for things to change ... at least until you arrive and have finally set up your kitchen.

—*Diana Ringquist*

A WORD ABOUT FAMILY LEFT BEHIND

*"Ohana means family. Family means no one
gets left behind or forgotten."*
—*Lilo and Stitch* (2002)

Unfortunately, part of the military and foreign service lifestyle means that family does get left behind. Parents, siblings, extended family, and if you stay in the service long enough, children are all left behind. This can be difficult or easy depending on the relationship, but when they really need you it can be heart-wrenching to be far away.

Technology has helped us bridge the gap tremendously. FaceTime, Skype, and other face-to-face live interaction software, VOIPs, VPNs, online ordering, Postagram, Snapfish, and innumerable other companies help us keep our families up to date with the latest developments in our lives. Great as they are, there are times when they just can't meet the needs of the situation.

Start now to talk with your family about long-term plans and concerns. Do your parents have a will, a durable power of attorney for health care, a power of attorney? Who will take care of them in an emergency and long-term? What resources are available in their community to help? What about your siblings? What are their plans? What about you? These are not easy discussions, but they are critically important. I hope you will never need to use any of these documents, but if and when you do, having them will be a blessing and remove some of the stress from your plate.

Knowing my mother's wishes from our conversations over the years allowed me to make her end-of-life decisions with her wishes in mind so she could die with as much dignity as possible and I could mourn my loss and not beat myself up over my choices for her.

—*Diana Ringquist*

PLEASE EXPLAIN WHERE YOU'RE FROM AGAIN

It's a long-standing joke among Military folk to have to explain where you're from during a PCS move.

Originally from Indiana, my army husband and I established Tennessee residency while at Fort Campbell, and kept it there through many moves. When orders came to move from Fort Riley, Kansas, to Fort Lee, Virginia, we found ourselves in an awkward predicament as we had unwittingly let our Tennessee residency lapse.

When our home sold that summer, we literally had no home, no address, and no official residency—homeless.

I spent the next two months visiting family before driving out to Virginia to join my husband. When family introduced me to their friends and neighbors, it was never more difficult to explain where we were from. At one such introduction, to avoid another long story, I simply said, "I'm from Virginia," thinking that would be the end of it.

The unsuspecting lady continued, "Oh, how do you like Virginia?"

My awkward confession came after a short pause, "Actually, I've never been there." This left her speechless. It was a simple question, but the answer was complicated.

I have found it helpful to record all our addresses and time spent at each in the very front of my address book. You never know when you might need to recall when and where you lived, or maybe even on the not-so-rare occasion, where you currently live.

LIFE HACK

Keep a record of all your own home addresses and timelines in your address book.

—*Diane Campbell*

Author's Note: You'll need a record of all your addresses, dates, and landlords' info for certain security clearances. This is important, especially after so many moves!

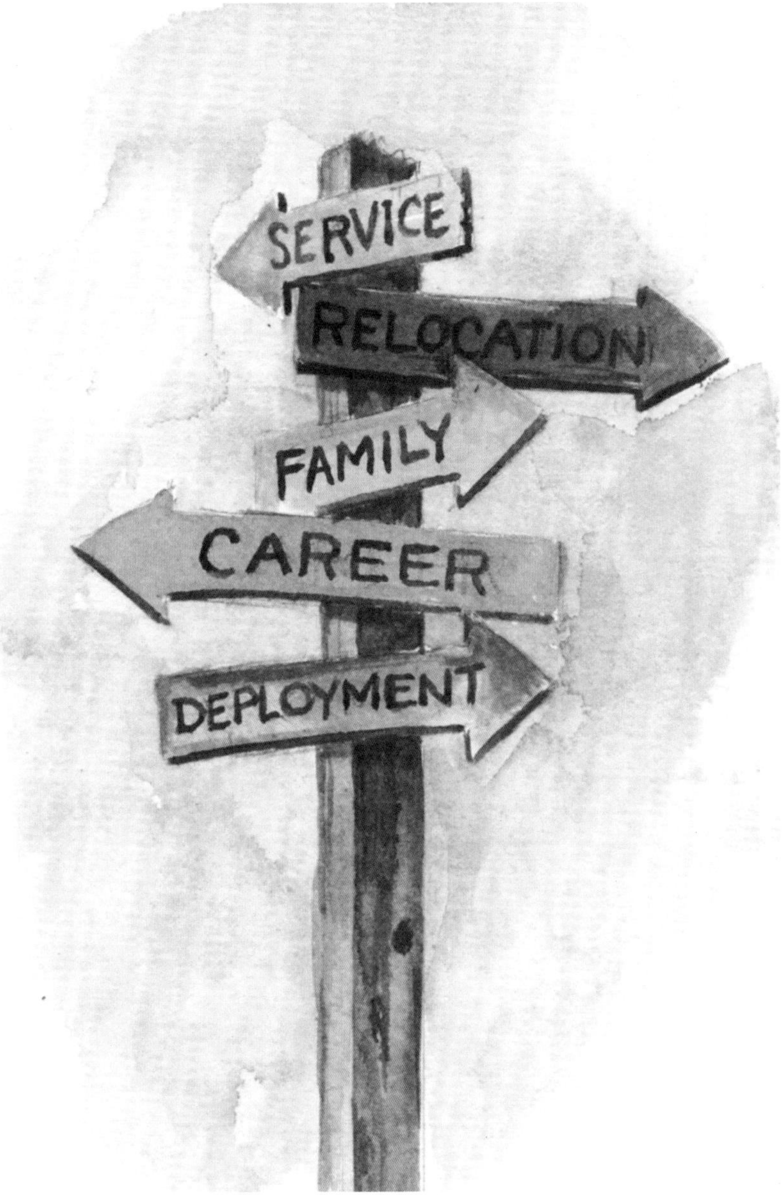
SERVICE
RELOCATION
FAMILY
CAREER
DEPLOYMENT

PART 6

Having/Not Having a Career while Mil-spousing

KEEPING YOUR CAREER ON TRACK

One of the biggest issues we see facing military spouses is trying to balance the military lifestyle with long-term employment. Most civilian employers don't really understand the challenges we face as military spouses and, many times, once they hear you are a military spouse, they smile and thank you, and you never hear from them again, because they see you as already moving before the interview is complete.

Although, there are employers out there who get you, and not only do they get you, you are actually a valuable commodity to them. I'm talking about those who work in and with the federal government.

Military spouses bring a valuable skill set to the table for the government and contractors that is hard to come by: an insider's knowledge of the military. Leverage that knowledge and apply it in careers associated with the military.

In my case, I was a recent college grad with a degree in English. Not really knowing what I was going to do with it, or how I was going to manage getting a job with a known PCS on the horizon, I applied for a position at a small army newspaper as a reporter.

My understanding of the military and rank structure landed me the job because I was able to hit the ground running with no learning curve. I already knew the programs and acronyms, giving me a leg up on the competition, and almost all of my superiors were either active duty, civilians who had once been active duty, or spouses themselves.

These were people who *got* me! We understood one another's lifestyles, and they weren't afraid of the inevitable PCS. Once I was on the team at the paper, I started being asked to help out with other things in the public affairs office, such as tours, training service members on how to interact with the media, and community relations.

That was more than twenty years ago, and I have maintained my career and progressed from a newbie staff writer to being a director of entire communications efforts at multi-star levels within the Department of Defense, and all along the way I have met people who valued not only my professional experience, but also the life experiences I have gained as a military spouse living around the world.

Almost every career specialty can be found working with or in the federal government—you just have to find your specialty niche.

LIFE HACK

Find your career equivalent in federal service or contracting.

—Staci-Jill Burnley

GET BUSY

Your spouse is in the military? Fact: you will fly solo. A lot. While it's easy to focus on the flaws with this scenario, resist! That mentality gets you nowhere. Think of it as a *Choose Your Own Adventure* book. What have you always wanted to achieve? Do it! And stick with it.

There are loads of resources for military spouses for education and career assistance. Other ideas—join a running club, volunteer (hospitals, retirement homes, schools, libraries, churches, food banks, animal shelters, to name a few), organize your home, learn to play a musical instrument, take a language course.

You are part of the "team" allowing your spouse to serve our country. In order to be a solid player you have to care for yourself. I realize kids and other major commitments may impact your ability to pursue your wildest dreams but keep in mind, one of the greatest gifts you can give your children is allowing them to see you succeed.

Whether you earn a college degree, certification, land a new job, or adopt a new art hobby, you will not only reap the benefits of your accomplishments, but you will have made time go by at lightning speed.

—Anonymous

"Big Red" Needle Felted on Linen by Carol Van Drie
Photo credit: Steve Dean, Lansing, Michigan

PORTABLE INTERNET HOTSPOTS AND VPNS IN THE WORLD OF CYBERSECURITY

The Internet has become an integral part of our daily lives. In the midst of a PCS, there is almost always a period of time between cancellation of your old service and set up of your new service. Free Wi-Fi and unlimited data plans become your best friends at this point, but staying cyber-safe is not always something we think about first. Free Wi-Fi is not secure, even if you must ask for the password. Without a password, it means anyone anywhere within range can get on the network and can access anyone on the network. With a password, it means anyone with the password can get on the network and can access anyone on the network. Consider this when weighing the pros and cons of getting online. Practice good cyber-hygiene and check for a password, ask how often the password is changed, and use anti-virus/anti-malware software on all your devices—including your phone! Remember, if it connects to the Internet, it is vulnerable.

Portable Internet Hotspots are a reasonably priced alternative to Free Wi-Fi and are available in some form almost everywhere. These devices may be a small accessory that you can pay-as-you-go or set up a plan. Many smartphones can also perform this function. Take the time before you are in the middle of a move to learn more. If possible, ask your sponsor at the new assignment if they can work to arrange your Internet service before your arrival or provide you with information so you can begin the process early.

Regardless of how you choose to connect to the Internet, do some research into anti-virus/anti-malware software. Choose what best fits your needs, download it, and use it at all times! Set your devices to auto-update so you can have the latest protection for your software. Consider using a VPN (virtual private network) which can be used at-will to protect your location and give you access when overseas. Pay attention to the websites you use, emails you receive, and pop-ups. If you do not think you are a target, that makes you the perfect target!

—Diana Ringquist

BREAKING INTO FEDERAL EMPLOYMENT

There are definitely benefits to being a federal employee: great insurance options for health, dental, and vision that give you options outside of or in addition to Tricare, good retirement plan, and awesome resources for work/life balance. You'd think everyone would like to be a "govvie."

The biggest trick most people face seems to be actually getting hired as a federal employee. I won't lie—landing a government job can be more mysterious than where all the missing socks go in the dryer, and as random as who gets struck by lightning, but military spouses *do* have an edge when it comes to making some magic happen and helping the stars align for an advantageous outcome in getting that coveted government job.

To support military spouses in advancing their careers despite the frequent relocations required by military life, the Department of Defense has expanded employment opportunities for military spouses. The key is knowing the programs out there available *only* to military spouses, and that are designed to boost your profile and get you noticed over others competing for the same job.

Military Spouse Preference applies when positions are filled using competition procedures and the spouse is determined to be among the best qualified. This program is derived from Title 10, USC, Section 1784, "Employment Opportunities for Military Spouses," and applies to spouses of active-duty military members of the US Armed Forces (including the Coast Guard), who relocate to accompany their sponsor on a PCS move.

There is also Executive Order 13473 which affords expedited recruitment and selection of spouses of members of the Armed Forces for appointment to positions in the competitive service of the federal civil service. This was the way I entered federal service and was hired by the Department of Labor at the GS-14 level.

Another big perk for working military spouses is the newly revamped Military Spouse Residency Relief Act (MSRRA) that provides protection to military spouses related to residency, voting, and taxes. The MSRRA amends the Servicemembers Civil Relief Act (SCRA) to include the same privileges to a military servicemember's spouse.

This had a huge financial benefit for our family by allowing me to pay state income tax in my service member's home of record state, which had lower state taxes than the state we were living and working in.

There are new and changing programs to solely benefit military spouse employment being implemented all the time, and it pays to be knowledgeable and current on them if you are looking at starting or continuing your career.

—*Staci-Jill Burnley*

LIFE HACK

Know the ins and outs of special hiring initiatives and other career benefits for working military spouses.

Author's Note: This is this contributor's personal experience. As laws and executive orders can change, always check for the current status or version. A local civilian employment office is a good resource for current law or you can visit www.MilitaryOneSource.mil for specific military spouse employment information.

FINDING YOUR "THING"

"I'm pretty sure I have more tea than the British Consulate!"
—ME

I love tea. This is an understatement. I am obsessed with tea! Black tea, white tea, green tea, Rooibos tea, herbal tea, fruit tea, yellow tea, citrus tea, blended tea, flavored tea, the list goes on and on!

I learned to love tea from my mother. She was a lovely woman who made tea every day for our family's four o'clock "Teatime" when we would gather for a cup of tea (milk for the children) and a small snack. She held this tradition as a means of tiding us over until dinner.

My mother made the worst tea. Despite her loving and practical intention, two bags of tea in a large pot of water makes tinted water, not tea. When I discovered one teabag was meant for one cup of water, the world of tea opened up and I was hooked! Tea became my "thing."

I have moved my tea and tea paraphernalia across multiple states, six countries, and three continents. My tea has been given as gifts to foreign dignitaries who are thrilled to receive it, shared with host and third-country nationals, offered to family and friends, and sipped quietly alone. No matter where I have gone, short trip or PCS move, my tea has gone with me.

You may not be a fan of tea, and I will not hold that against you. You do, however, need to find "your thing." Find a thing that represents "home," gives you comfort, and is relatively portable. Do you love poetry? A book of poetry purchased by you or received as a gift is something you can throw in your bag. Do you have a favorite craft that is relatively small and contained? Cross-stitch or jewelry making with a travel-sized tool kit may be a good option, whereas stained glass design requires a lot of space and equipment. Is makeup or pretty nails your go-to? Find your one thing, make sure it is portable and can be taken on airplanes, and pack it today!

En route to your new home, you could be delayed. Upon arrival, your home may not yet be ready to move into, or there could be a mix-up with your luggage.

Once moved in, bad days will happen regardless of where you live. Homesickness, loneliness, and culture shock are very real experiences. These are times for a little self-care and self-love. Apply your beloved nail color with extra attention. Try that new winged eyeliner look. Read a few poems from your favorite book. Make a new pair of earrings or complete the next section in your latest cross-stitch.

Take the time to boil the water, add the scoop, set the timer, remove the strainer, and enjoy your lovely cup of tea. Breathe deeply and know that things will get better.

—Diana Ringquist

THE "LOVE-ME" BOOK

The Love-Me book is a fantastic tradition that everyone should follow! Service members are taught to keep one, but spouses and children rarely do. A Love-Me book is a simple binder in which you keep all your records of your successes and achievements. These can be certificates, recommendations, degrees, transcripts, awards, memberships, ribbons, memorabilia of any type that remind you of your accomplishments.

The purpose is two-fold. First, a Love-Me book reminds us of how great we are and how awesome we can be. Children achieve and quickly move on to the next activity or grade and the achievement is quickly forgotten. Spouses do far more than is generally recognized and it is easy to downplay your achievements as your service member and children rack up the awards and recognition.

Having this reminder can be important when facing the challenges associated with military life. The other reason to have and maintain your Love-Me book is if you decide to seek employment or return to school. Your Love-Me book gives you the documentation to support your resume or application.

—*Diana Ringquist*

MAKING FRIENDS AFTER PCS WHEN YOU'RE A WORKING MOM

Living the military life means I've made several wonderful groups of friends over the years, with whom I regularly connect by phone, Zoom, Facetime, other social media, etc. On the other hand, moving frequently means I'm always the new kid on the block, trying to fit into groups of friends whose kids have known each other since preschool.

Sometimes, I wilt at the idea of starting all over again making new friends, when I know I'm leaving again in a few years or less—it's hard! But I'm the kind of person who just needs people, so usually I find my stiff upper lip and reach out somehow.

I have found that even during times when my professional workload was heavy and my days were jam-packed, I could find a way to volunteer at the kids' schools. Shelving books in the library or helping a PTA committee plan family events has helped me connect to other parents. It's also been a great way to stay relevant in my children's academic community, plus meeting other parents has turned into happy hours, book clubs, and backyard parties. Those friendships have kept me sane and grounded.

Bonus: Making new friends has also helped me discover a good network of babysitters so my husband and I can have date night!

—Heather Murphy Capps

HOME REPAIR KIT

Are you new to being a stay-at-home spouse? Thank goodness for the DIY revolution and sites like YouTube where you can learn to do just about anything around the house—home repair has never been easier! If you do not have a home repair kit, you are still at the mercy of waiting on someone else to take care of things you can easily knock out quickly and inexpensively.

We have probably all seen the little tool kits targeted to women—and those can be good starting points that you can expand upon to meet your needs—or you can make your own. You will need a durable container, either a thick canvas bag or the more traditional plastic or metal box. Consider things you know you will need and use the list below to help get you started.

Basics:
- Hammer
- Picture hanging kit (nails and wood screws of different sizes)
- Screwdrivers (regular and Phillips head)
- Tape measure (20- or 25-foot measure is always a safer bet)
- Pliers
- Level
- Utility knife with extra blades
- Painter's tape
- Packing tape
- Variety of felt, plastic, and carpet dots (often sold in variety packs and used for moving furniture and protecting walls/floors/surfaces)

Nice to have:
- Vise grip
- Wire cutters
- Cordless drill
- Cordless screwdriver
- Glues (wood, superglue, etc.)

- Pipe sealing kit (often sold as kits, you can also opt for a simple roll of plumber's tape)
- Drain snake
- Paintable stick-on wall repair kit

Although the average person is capable of hanging a new light, never attempt to rewire your home unless you are a licensed electrician. This is something best left to the professionals.

—Diana Ringquist

TRANSITIONS CAN BE POSITIVE

Never did I dream that I would be living this life.

Like many people, I lived the American dream. Working eight to five with a one-hour commute each way. Seeing my husband and baby for a rushed breakfast before daycare drop-off and a tired dinner before bedtime quiet. Because of the weekday grind, weekend quality time was filled with grocery shopping, laundry, and housework.

Just when the mundane started to become a robotic and a sad normal, I got the news that we were moving. It was go time.

There's nothing like packing up and picking up your whole life to give you a new sense of being. We were moving to a country I'd never heard of. Would be learning a language I knew I'd never master. Facing day-to-day challenges I'd never forget. I was scared, but I had purpose. The familiar mundane became the past, and the unknown became the exciting future.

Once we arrived in this very foreign land, I found a new way of living. I was no longer the breadwinner; I was now the trailing spouse. Now I could spend time with my family, cook dinner, and do fun things over the weekend. Every day for the next two years brought something different.

This door of world exploration opened and I saw how refreshing change can be. The knowledge that after two years, just when routine sets in and life becomes normal, we will get word of our next destination and our next set of challenges. Our life will change again, and probably will continue to do so for the foreseeable future until we decide to make it stop.

PCSing is life-changing in so many ways. There is constant adventure and excitement and a great sense of awakening. For me it was redefining. It killed my career as I knew it, but it saved my marriage. It forced us to grow as a family and learn what our new normal looked like. I could see a new role for myself as a spouse, homemaker, and mother. I liked what I saw and am grateful for this wild life we live.

—*Victoria Griffith*

MAKE THE MOST OF YOUR WEIGHT LIMIT
WHEN YOU MOVE

Army spouses have a tough go when it comes to professional stability. Let's be real: moving every two years (or less) is a rocky road for anyone trying to build a local client base or get promoted within an organization.

I am fortunate in that I have a portable profession, and am self-employed. In addition to being able to maintain consistency wherever I live, I also have my own office. And because what I do for a living is write, and teach writing to other adults, I have a lot of books. I mean, a *lot* of heavy reference books.

Being self-employed is equally helpful when it comes time to PCS—because the weight limits for household goods increase when you are factoring in a spouse's home office.

I figured that out on our last move when it was clear we were going to max out our weight limits and end up having to pay out of pocket for every over-limit pound we put in the mover's truck. My husband had received a promotion, so our weight limit increased since the last move, but of course our kids got older too, which meant our *stuff* had multiplied exponentially as well. Sigh.

But then . . . I looked at the fine print. And I discovered that there is such thing as an additional allowable weight for a spouse's home office: furniture, gear, and supplies.

If this applies to you, do the happy dance, as I did. Then, label your home office and point that out to the packers so they will label the boxes accordingly as well. Easier in the unpacking phase, too!

—*Heather Murphy Capps*

DUPLICATE TRICARE DOCUMENTS FOR EMERGENCIES

In the fall of 2014, we were living on the East Coast. It was late in my pregnancy. Some might not know, but Tricare requires you to have a referral for maternity care and a separate one for labor and delivery.

During my 38th week of pregnancy, Hurricane Sandy was barreling up the Eastern Seaboard. My husband, an Air Force pilot, was sent to evacuate aircraft from the path of the hurricane. This left me alone, 38 weeks pregnant, with a toddler, a dog, my husband's prized Scotch collection, and the recommendation from my physician to evacuate.

So inland I went, but bringing my Tricare documents was the last thing on my mind. I also didn't have my portal password. So an already-stressful hotel stay was made even more so when I realized that if I went into labor, a mountain of paperwork would further complicate matters.

Fortunately, the baby had the courtesy to wait until we were back home. I delivered our son at our local hospital with my husband at my side.

Since this experience, I always keep duplicate documents of our referrals in our emergency documents file and online cloud storage. I might forget our emergency file but I will always have my phone to pull up documents. Oh, and my husband thoroughly enjoyed his government sponsored "hardship" aircraft evacuation to Orlando.

LIFE HACK

Always keep duplicates and email copies of Tricare documents and referrals in your emergency files.

—Lauren Walsh

MEDICAL KITS

In the mid-2010s, my service member and I stared at the deep gash on our friend's head. Having been trained as a medic, my service member was officially the highest medically trained person at the assignment at the time and had been called to assist.

"It's going to need stitches," my service member said grimly.

"Don't worry, he knows what he's doing," I assured our friend.

She was one of three emergencies our family responded to during our time at that assignment. I've never been happier for my reasonably well-stocked first aid kit that I check through regularly.

There are lots of medical kits on the market, which can be overwhelming. Consider where you're going, what medical care is available there, and also the specific needs of your family. If you are going to a base in the United States that provides full medical care to spouses and families with a 24-hour Emergency Department, you'll need a smaller kit than if you are going to an overseas posting where a nurse practitioner is the highest trained person available, only during limited hours, and significant medical needs and dental issues require a medical evacuation (MEDEVAC). If someone in your family needs a rescue inhaler, epi-pen, insulin injections, or similar specific needs, then you have additional items to consider.

Even if you don't have children, your neighbors might. I always encourage medical kits that can be used for adults and kids alike. This can be as simple as fun band aids or as advanced as remembering to include a pediatric blood pressure cuff. I like to throw in a small pack of crayons or colored pencils and a coloring book for kids because it can be a good distraction if a parent gets hurt.

Whatever you choose for your family's medical kit, be certain you know how to use the contents safely and properly. Set a reminder on your phone or in your planner to check through the contents for expired or depleted supplies. Whenever possible, take a class on first aid and/or CPR. You never know when you might need these skills and the best medical kit in the world does not provide care.

—*Diana Ringquist*

NETWORKING 101

Networking. Even though this term can have a negative stigma, it is a part of life, especially military life. This hack is simple. Send out Christmas cards. It keeps your active duty military spouse connected to all his/her old commanders, keeps you top of mind, and keeps a professional network going for times outside of the military.

Everyone in the military is connected, and people tend to forget that. Also, the active military persons usually aren't the greatest at networking, and this is where the spouse can really pick up the slack by taking on the extra effort to collect addresses and keep an up-to-date database of names and addresses as they move.

Remember, as much as we don't like to admit it, the spouse is a reflection of our active duty counterpart, and this is a fun way to serve behind the scenes with a lasting impact!

—Lesley Gagnon

RESOURCE AND PERSPECTIVE THAT ARE INVALUABLE!

I am a female spouse. I cannot begin to say anything about the experiences that male spouses have and the unique challenges they face.

What I can say is this: these men have a remarkable and unique perspective on our shared experience that is invaluable, and they are tremendous resources to us and our community.

Do your best to remember that male spouses are not only part of our community, but that we need to make the effort to ensure they are included and welcomed.

—Diana Ringquist

PART 7

Keeping Kids Connected/ Contained

FAMILY TRADITIONS REIGN SUPREME

When asked where they are from, my children have declared to complete strangers that they are Belizean, which makes some sense as we were actually posted in Belize. My favorite declaration was when my three-year-old daughter said she was Chinese, where we have never served or even visited.

Clearly, there has been some confusion among my offspring about their nationality. In order to maintain a connection to our roots, we make extra efforts to keep our American traditions alive and remind our kids where their family is from.

Halloween is always a family favorite in our house, and ours is more often than not the only one on the block covered in spooky spiders. After weeks of deliberations and consultations with The Master Carver (a.k.a. my husband) we find whatever carvable orb is available, as pumpkins aren't always available where you'll be stationed. It turns out watermelons and pineapples are just as effective as pumpkins. We also strive to end the night being known on the streets as the house with the best candy, proudly handing out our favorite American treats.

Overseas, Thanksgiving is generally not a local holiday, so even though the kids usually have school, we opt to keep them home as if we were in the States. They love letting their friends know they will not be in school on the fourth Thursday in November because they are Americans.

We do our very best to import some family, secure a roastable bird, and despite not always having the right ingredients available locally and frequently forgetting to order that canned pumpkin in time, we do our best to prepare a traditional meal that will feed us for days. We always go around the table saying what we're most thankful for, and always talk about playing "American" football, though that rarely happens.

Growing up, the Kentucky Derby was always celebrated among family and friends. We keep that tradition alive by having a party every year to watch the race. Big hats, fascinators, and seersucker suits are donned by our guests, many of whom have never even heard of the Kentucky Derby. The kids look forward to this and are eager to explain what a jockey silk is, which horse is their favorite, and to steering the other kids away from the Bourbon Balls.

We've made sure to incorporate American traditions into our life overseas so that still it becomes part of our family lore, and roots our children's identities in the culture from where they descend. Our home countries change, our houses change, our friends and schools change, but in this family, there will always be a special meal served on Thanksgiving, costumes and jack-o-lanterns on Halloween, and bourbon and big hats for the Kentucky Derby!

—*Meredith Farington*

PLUGGING IN WHEN YOU LIVE OFF POST

We're a Title 10 Army family—in other words, full-time Army National Guard. In other words, all the joy of being in the Army but none of the housing. To be honest, we're pretty okay with that. That said, plugging into well-established neighborhoods where we're the only military family—and where people live for lifetimes instead of one- to three-year stretches—can be daunting. Sometimes we envy our colleagues living on post where everyone understands our peripatetic lives.

When the kids were little and we didn't have school as a way to provide instant community in a new posting, I'd sign them up right away for community center music classes like "Music Together" or "Kindermusik." I loved it as much as the kids did because:

- it was fun;
- it was a chance to meet other parents;
- some of those connections turned into post-class playground playdates, and some even progressed to real friendship after that.

My kids have aged out of those music classes now, but they still remember taking them and they still know those songs by heart!

—*Heather Murphy Capps*

HELPING KIDS ADJUST

We have moved internationally a couple of times with preschool/young school-aged children and have been worried about the long-term effects of uprooting. So we've developed a couple of traditions that have helped make the transition easier for our kids.

First, before the move we try to make sure we take lots of pictures of them—of their favorite places to play, with friends and family, around our house, at school. Then we use these to make a photo album to give to the kids so they can look at it if they are feeling upset, missing people, or just want to remember their time in a particular place.

Second, we ask their teachers if they can have some special time set aside on their last day to talk about the move, sharing pictures or postcards or fun facts we might have about where we are moving. We also bring in an edible treat (if possible) and a small token gift to hand out. Attached to the gift we include our new contact information.

The kids are usually very excited to "show and tell" with their classmates about their new home and it's usually a big hit with the class. By including the contact information the kids have also made some pen or video-chat pals, which also helps maintain a sense of connection from place to place.

—*Jackie Cooper*

TALK!

Children have an idea about what is going on, even if you don't tell them everything. They live in your home, after all! By involving your child/children in PCS, TDY, and deployment planning and strategies, you have the ability to lessen their (and your) anxiety, develop a better understanding of their perspectives, create more honest and open communication with them, and engage them in the process in a positive and proactive manner. Addressing concerns early gives everyone time to find information, develop strategies together, and adjust to the inevitable changes.

Find ways to keep the fun in the process. For PCSing, creating moving-box forts or unpacking scavenger hunts can keep the giggles going, lessen stress, and create positive memories. Working together to plan surprises to mail or slip into the luggage of the TDY or deployed service member can be exciting. Paper chains to mark time until return can give a sense that time is moving even when it feels as though it is taking "forever."

Allow yourself and your kids to be creative. Think of and share ways to ensure old connections are maintained while new ones are created. Perhaps you and your family would like to make a memory book or a version of the "Memory" card game that features friends, family members, or places you enjoyed. Having a regular time to call or video with those far away gives everyone something to look forward to with anticipation.

No matter what, enlist your child/children into the process. Give them the space and security of knowing that whatever they are feeling is okay, and sharing it is a great way to feel heard and validated. Share how you are feeling as well and be able to admit when you have handled your emotions poorly. This allows them to watch their favorite role models manage feelings and situations and helps them learn how to manage their own.

—*Diana Ringquist*

INTENTIONAL TIME WITH KIDS

When my husband deployed, we had just given birth to our first child. He got to know his newborn daughter for only eight days and then he was off! I had a lot of time to think about what a healthy transition would be for him when he comes back and enters a world where he is now a father on a routine basis. Our baby would have no idea who he was, and that can be awkward and totally difficult for anyone to handle, no less a soldier who just came back from combat.

One idea that I kept hearing from many spouses whom I respected, was to give him time alone with the child to get to know her without me hovering over them. He needed to figure out how to be a father, and I cannot control or advise him how to do this.

So, after a couple of weeks of him getting settled, I purposely left the house to run errands, hang with friends, twice a week for at least a couple of hours. Then, when I felt the time was right, I left for an entire weekend! When I came back, the two of them were inseparable, and it's been history ever since.

My ultimate recommendation (especially now that we have four kids) would be to absolutely schedule for your spouse to have alone time with each child. A child changes *a lot* whether in six months or eighteen, and the best way for your spouse to figure that out is intentional time with them!

—*Allison Wood*

CREATING FAMILY TRADITIONS

Soon after it was published in 1929, my father acquired the little book *One Hundred and One Famous Poems*. He was twenty-one. It had a soft leather-like cover, and was 5 x 8 inches and just shy of ½-inch thick, so it could curve to match one's rear pocket. If not in his hip pocket, it stayed in a special place where it was easily accessible. I'm not sure of all the circumstances when he would pull it out to give him a bit of needed courage, or to enrich his life. Wordsworth, Keats, Poe, Kipling, Oliver Wendell Holmes . . . their rhythmic phrasing became part of him.

"Daddy, Daddy, please read to us," we'd beg after dinner. He would push away from the dining room table or we'd cuddle up next to him on the couch, and he'd launch into Eugene Field's *Little Boy Blue*:

> "The little toy dog is covered with dust,
> But sturdy and staunch he stands . . ."

To be followed by Mary Howitt's *The Spider and the Fly*:
"'Will you walk into my parlor?' said the spider to the fly;
'Tis the prettiest little parlor that you ever did spy . . .'"

As we grew older, his selections spoke to our levels of understanding. Daddy's voice would ring out with Longfellow's *Hiawatha's Childhood*:

> "By the shores of Gitche Gumee,
> By the shining Big-Sea-Water,
> Stood the wigwam of Nokomis . . ."

And my favorite, Alfred Noyes's *The Highwayman*:
"The wind was a torrent of darkness among the gusty trees,
The moon was a ghostly galleon tossed upon cloudy seas,
The road was a ribbon of moonlight over the purple moor,
And the highwayman came riding,
Riding, riding,
The highwayman came riding, up to the old inn-door . . ."

When I was recuperating from polio, my father brought me a little present, my own copy of the little brown book. I was thrilled to have one of these anthologies of my own. It brought me comfort as I struggled to cope with this sickness which had crippled my Daddy when he was my age, only sixteen.

The book went to college with me and remained one of my most prized possessions as the years passed. During a hard time as a teacher when a colleague blamed me for doing some bad things she had done, I went home and pulled out my little book. I remembered a poem my father had read many years before which hadn't meant much then, *If,* by Rudyard Kipling. It strengthened me to keep my calm.

> "If you can keep your head when all about you
> Are losing theirs and blaming it on you;
> If you can trust yourself when all men doubt you,
> But make allowance for their doubting too . . .
> If you can fill the unforgiving minute
> With sixty seconds' worth of distance run,
> Yours is the Earth and everything that's in it,
> And—which is more—you'll be a Man, my son!
> (I quickly changed it to—*you'll be a Woman, my dear!*)

My children also curled up to hear their grandfather recite their favorites. After he passed, I found his original copy. Last month as I thought of a birthday present for my dear grandson, Zach, I knew he would treasure his great grandfather's original book.

My daughter was brought to tears. She knew what it had meant to me over the years. Many of the same poems and others had been read to her, and she had read them herself. When she and both her children retired that night, they spent a long time going over her favorites.

Military children may not have the continuity of a family home, but they can still have a strong sense of home and family by having traditions and mementos like this, passed down through generations.

—*Susie Doyle*

SCHOOL RECORDS WORKBOOK

Our kids typically have the experience of moving every few years. Beyond the need to have skills in making new friends and adapting to new places, our children face the sometimes-daunting task of integrating into a new school system. Integration goes beyond the social aspects and superficial demands of the school schedule. Jumping between states, DODEA and public or private schools, homeschooling, international schools, and host-nation schools requires our children to make large changes in their expectations and performance.

One thing we can do as parents to help children is to develop and maintain a School Records Workbook for each child. It can be tremendously helpful to you, your child, and the teachers. A School Records Workbook starts with a three-ring binder—I would suggest dividers as well to help you stay organized. Create sections as appropriate based on whatever applies to you and your child. You can start with the following topics or check online for premade printables to shortcut this step:

- New Student Checklist/Departing Student Checklist
- Required Registration Information
- Birth Certificate
- Immunization Record
- Social Security Card
- Legal Paperwork
- Medical Records; Health Information
- Doctors' Reports/Sports Physical
- Food/Environmental Allergies
- Medications
- Progress Reports, Report Cards, Transcripts
- Standardized Testing Results (ITBS, COGAT, Iowa, 504, Benchmark, PSAT, etc.)
- Class Schedule, Textbook Information, Class Syllabus (from previous school)

- Student Biographical Information/Assessments
- Portfolio
- Teacher Assessments
- Letters of Recommendation
- Parent Assessments
- Evaluations (most current in front)
- Admissions, Review, and Dismissal Board (ARD)
- Individualized Education Program (IEP)
- Individualized Family Service Plan (IFSP)
- Advanced Placement Classes/IB Program
- Outside Therapies (as appropriate)
- Community Service, Service Learning, Volunteer Activities
- Sports and Electives
- Awards/Certificates
- Previous School Information (keep for each school/educational program)
- Release of Information/Records
- Name, Address, Phone Number, Point of Contact
- Business Card for Point of Contact/other important individuals
- Miscellaneous Records

—Diana Ringquist

INTERNET AND SOCIAL MEDIA

Only you as a parent can decide what is right for your child. This is especially true with regard to the Internet and social media. There is absolutely no "one right answer" for every family, let alone for every child. How your child can keep up with their friends from move to move is something you and your family must discuss and decide.

This can sometimes lead to differing opinions and disagreements. Keep in mind that not every child (military, foreign service, or civilian) uses social media. Although there is more and more pressure to use social media seemingly coming from every source to include our children's schools, with new platforms being developed all the time, it does not mean your children should have unfettered access.

Talk to your child's school and any extracurricular activities. Find out their communication policy for sharing important information with you as a parent, as well as with your child. This serves two important purposes. First, it eliminates you as the parent having to look in multiple locations for information. Second, as a minor your child should not have any communication or accounts that you are not aware of and cannot monitor.

If this is the case with any school or activity, bring your concerns to the attention of the principal or director immediately. You should always have full access to and control of your child's Internet history and social media accounts, and you should have a clear and agreed upon means of communication with those in whom you trust your child's care and education.

—*Diana Ringquist*

TRAVELING IN EUROPE WITH CHILDREN

Take the Kids! Travel often . . . but have realistic expectations!

While living in Europe, people always asked us, "How do you travel so many places with four children under the age of eight?"

The answer was and is simple: realistic expectations! I remember one of our first trips in Europe. We were in Nice, France, with three children under four years old. After a full day exploring the city, my husband insisted we go to a really nice restaurant in Garibaldi Square. I was totally against this idea because I knew someone was going to have a meltdown.

Sure enough, our youngest had had enough. The experience was a disaster—the baby screamed during the entire meal. We were forced to cut the meal short, and when we returned to our hotel she immediately calmed down. We learned a valuable lesson that day: children have limits and it's easy to overstimulate them.

Later, we came to realize that we could travel almost anywhere with our children as long as our expectations were reasonable. You can still dine at that restaurant, but might need to go at 5:00 p.m. instead of 8:00 p.m. It also may be prudent to skip the two-hour walking tour in favor of a custom-made tour you create from your own research.

Finally, a trip to a park is always recommended; some of my children's best memories were created in spontaneous park detours. If you give your children a taste of wanderlust, they will become lifelong explorers. Know your children's limits and beware of late-night dinners at French restaurants.

—*Lauren Walsh*

WHEN TO PRETEND YOUR CHILD HAS DIABETES

My name is Meredith and I'm a terrible liar. No really, it's bad. Anyone can see directly through me immediately if I don't 100 percent believe exactly what I'm saying. It's a quality I both love and hate about myself, but you work with what you've got, right?

Military service has been a part of my family for pretty much as long as the United States has been a thing. I had ancestors on both sides of the Civil War, medics on the ground in WWI, and while my mom claims I'm not named for the ship her uncle went down in, in WWII, he wasn't on the USS *Jessica*.

My uncle served on submarines in the Korean War and my grandfather became a mustang officer as the Midway was going down in Leyte Gulf. He spent the rest of his 27-year career on a carrier deck and told me some killer stories when I was a kid.

Me falling in love with a pilot? A delightful inevitability. Especially considering that my husband was concealed in his mom's belly for a full eight months before her flight surgeon realized why her flight suit was getting tight around the middle and grounded her.

Yep, my MIL helped pave the way for gals to land on carriers during a period of history when women were often only in hangars during change of command ceremonies, wrangling children into being invisible when a guest speaker still had seventeen more bullet points to articulate.

I mean, there is an art to it.

Which brings me to my hack: Pretend Diabetes. To this day, I don't understand why children are sometimes encouraged to come to Change of Command ceremonies. I've been to more than I'd like to count. They're always scheduled around 10:00 a.m. on a Thursday. Exactly when any mobile child who isn't in school needs to either be going down for a nap or getting their wiggles out at the park before lunch.

From Chief to Commodore, if your spouse is anyone's boss, gracefully bowing out of the event is frowned upon, especially if you've just checked in.

If this is your first rodeo, a COC starts with coffee, cookies, donuts, and some sort of punch with a giant Bundt-pan-shaped ice cube in the middle. "It's made of Sprite! Dontcha know? Aren't the bubbles fun?!" It won't have vodka, unfortunately. The quiet murmur of mingling and finding a seat is an allocated delay. Once that's settled, everyone is expected to sit down and be quiet for the next two hours until a reception begins that lasts the rest of the weekend.

You'll be there in white pants or a tea-length dress, hoping no one sees the avocado stain at the hem from a rushed breakfast. You'll either be a new mom or have at least one child under three wearing clothing that probably should have been ironed. Oops. You're kind of new to the squadron and won't remember more than twelve of the 416 people you're about to be introduced to. You'll hope that goes both ways.

The tiny human you love will see the cookie table. They'll see other children with cookies. You silently panic. You've never given your nearly-two-year-old daughter sugar because your grandmother died from diabetes and it's something you're actually, for real, worried about. She does pee a lot . . . Is it a legitimate fear? Probably not. But your friends love you anyway and make special veggie muffins that look like cupcakes at birthday parties so you can lie to your child for a little bit longer.

How can you get out of this without your normally well-behaved child making a scene? The cookies do look amazing. Can you avoid the table? Redirect? Shouldn't there be a plane to go look at? Yes. Yes, there is.

Except now, the incoming CO's wife has caught your eye. She smiles at you, brightly and sincerely. You've met her once before, she's actually awesome. As she makes her way over to welcome you with a hug, complete with a knowing eye-roll about the whole event, she holds out a perfectly iced cookie that couldn't have come from a store. Did she actually make all 500 of them?

Before you can even think about it, "I'm so sorry but we're having [junior] tested for diabetes right now and it's stressing me out a bit" comes out of your mouth. Did you really just say that? Yep. Yep, ya did.

The savvy, knowing CO's wife slips the cookie away before your child sees it and ninja-snags a strawberry from a passing garnished drink tray to share with your delighted toddler. She winks and introduces you to another mom nearby.

"That was the most brilliant cookie escape I've ever seen. Pretend diabetes. Why didn't I think of that when my kids were toddlers? I'm Kate, a few other wives snuck wine into the wardroom. You have to tell them about this. Want to join me?"

Yes, new friend, yes I most certainly do.

—*Meredith Rummel*

Author's Note: We are aware diabetes is a serious chronic condition, and this humorous look at dealing with the emotional impact of the disease is in no way meant to make light of it.

ENGAGE KIDS IN THE MOVE, DECISION MAKING, AND TRADITIONS

You know that giving your child/children a say in basic decision making is important. When it comes to moving, the big decisions of when and where to move is largely out of your control, but giving kids a voice in the process helps to give them a sense of control and can help get their buy-in to the entire process.

Also, the attitude you take can determine how well the move goes and how smoothly the transition to your new life is made. This is equally true for your children. Engage them in basic decisions about their belongings. Offer creative opportunities with box forts and packing paper turned coloring paper or paper mâché crafts.

Depending on where you are moving, think in advance about holidays. If you always have a holiday tradition, consider if it is one you can maintain at your new home. A traditional dinner may not be appropriate if you are moving overseas to a country with certain food restrictions. Eggs may be difficult to find and it may be more difficult to find your favorite brand of dye.

Think about how you can purchase a live tree at your new assignment, or is it time to either buy a fake pine tree or learn to decorate a palm tree?

—*Diana Ringquist*

PART 8

Deployment and Redeployment, then Deployment Again

LEARN TO SAVOR THE TIME ALONE

If you are an introvert by nature, enjoying time alone may come more easily to you than it does to your extroverted counterparts. But as the days stretch into weeks and months, even introverts can feel the strain of missing your partner and friend.

Extroverts, with their love of time with others, may become the ones that excel as they tend to have a broad group of friends. Ultimately though, long and multiple deployments are a strain on individuals, couples, and families. Time alone, "single"-parenting, and "keeping the home fires burning" are usually a part of our experience and require some deft navigating.

Set some goals. Big ones are fine but break them down to month-by-month or even week-by-week. Set smaller monthly or weekly goals. It is fine to set daily goals as well. Find daily and weekly routines that bring you comfort. Set aside, guard, and regularly use your "me-time" and take care of yourself. If this seems selfish, remember, "If you don't take care of yourself first, you're no good to the rest of us!" —Barbara Stansberry

—*Diana Ringquist*

DIY AND LAWNCARE DURING A DEPLOYMENT

Not all of us are handy. I consider mowing, blowing, and edging the equivalent of my own personal hell (I doubt I am the only one).

Ever thrifty, I tried to save money by managing the maintenance of our large yard on my own, while my husband was deployed. I reasoned that my hate of yardwork would not exceed my love of the money that would be saved.

I failed to factor in the exhaustion of raising young children alone with no family in the area. I had a one-year-old who literally slept five hours a night and wouldn't take naps! I was dying of exhaustion.

Maintaining our yard became a nightmare. Every day, I would put my son in his crib, race outside to mow, edge, or blow one section. Being stubborn, I continued to do it myself, but it was an endless battle I never seemed to finish. Seven months later, my husband arrived home and said, "You should have hired someone!"

When spouses are deployed, we think we can do it all. It's okay to ask for help or, if finances permit: hire someone. The next time, if someone asked how they could help, I eagerly said, "Yes, could you come help with me the yardwork?"

LIFE HACK

Ask for help and invest in your sanity during long deployments.

—*Lauren Walsh*

FIND WAYS TO REMAIN ENGAGED

Modern technology and communication have eased some of the strain of being apart and wondering if your loved ones are safe and happy. There is always a balance between sharing the good and the bad of daily life with a deployed family member.

Determining what is enough information that everyone feels like part of the family and not so much that it causes worry and distraction is a unique challenge that every spouse must find.

It is important to determine how you will communicate and how often. If you have children, determine how the service member will stay engaged with them. Find out if it's possible to have a regular phone call or online visit. There are companies in the US that allow you to upload a photo and write a message to a postcard they will print and mail for you. Determine how you will handle holidays and special events. Care packages and handwritten letters and cards to service members far away are still as loved and enjoyed as they were a century or more ago. If you want to send homemade cookies, vacuum sealing them in smaller quantities of two to four keeps them fresher longer and can be easily shared with others who are feeling homesick.

Keep in mind, there are also pitfalls to our easy communication. Different countries have rules as to what can be sent. OPSEC (Operational Security) can be easily forgotten in the fast and immediate world of real-time communications. Think about what you say, write, and share. I have seen too many social media posts about how proud a spouse is of their military member, how much they love them, and how the military member will be deploying to X location on X day with X others by way of X means of transportation to do X job for X long. Loose lips may sink ships, but loose OPSEC can cost lives and missions.

—*Diana Ringquist*

MURPHY'S LAW

Definition: Anything that can go wrong will go wrong. When your spouse deploys, your world could potentially fall apart. The best advice I can give is prepare your mind ahead of time that though this likelihood is very common—mental preparation helps keep your sanity in check!

As long as you know and are expecting things like the refrigerator malfunctioning, car breaking down, flooded basement, insect infestation . . . I can go on, but you will probably be in a healthy mindset to handle these problems when they do arise, rather than having a nervous breakdown!

LIFE HACK

Be mentally prepared; there will be hard times.

—Jessi Burns

PRINCESSES NOT WELCOME HERE

That princess you might have been in high school or college does not mesh well in the military spouse world. Your active duty counterpart can be gone more than they are home some months or years, and things in your home/life might fall apart and you are the only one there to fix it.

Imagine you have dinner cooking, four hungry kids, and your garbage disposal suddenly makes a terrible sound and stops working, clogging your sink. You don't have time to call a plumber to check it out. Instead, as a military spouse, you now have to suppress any finicky tendencies you may have had, or relying on a brother or father, and roll up your sleeves and dig in that garbage disposal! You have to at least try to fix it!

Same thing when you're shopping at the PX and your kids leave every light inside your car on in broad daylight (so of course you don't realize it), and by the time you come back to the car, the battery is dead. Now, instead of keeping your kids waiting in a parking lot for a mechanic or Triple-A for potentially hours, you get out your own jumper cables, and ask the first person you see to help jump your car. Military spouses can't be scared to get a little dirty!

—Jessi Burns

THE BLESSING AND CURSE OF RETURN

We have all seen, if not experienced firsthand, that amazing moment when our service member returns after a deployment. It is thrilling, exciting, and a huge relief to have them home safe! Once again, you have your partner and your friend home with you, and you can be a family. This is a blessing, and now the work of reintegrating our lives can finally begin.

This is where the "curse" of the return can manifest, and it is not talked about nearly enough. Not only is it likely that your service member has changed due to experiences while deployed, but you have as well. You figured out how to run your home and your family without your partner, and now someone else wants a say in how things operate.

You may have become accustomed to sleeping alone and now there is another in your bed. You both may have had dreams and expectations of what it would be like to be together again, and reality is not living up to them. You may find that there are ways in which you are both strangers to each other. This can lead to serious relationship problems that may start at arrival or may take weeks or months to arise.

You are glad to be together, but you may also feel angry or frustrated with the other person. You may feel uncomfortable or even dismissed by a military culture that has copious resources for our military member and even our children but seems to overlook the military spouse.

Even our larger culture labels the person that leaves dirty underwear on the floor as a "hero" and you may feel ashamed that you find them and their behaviors to be irritating or maddening.

Take some time to get to know each other again. If you have children, this may be especially important to help them process this new person into their lives and for the service member to learn who this (now) "new" child is today.

Talk with each other and be honest about feelings and frustrations. Go back to dating for a while and explore how each of you has grown and changed. Explain how things are different and give your service member small ways to begin reintegrating into the family. This process can take months if the service member is staying for a long time or it can be a way to bridge the time between deployments that allows your main systems and routines to remain largely intact. Seek assistance if you are struggling individually, as a couple, or as a family. Over time, nearly everyone can rediscover their relationships.

Remember you were apart for much longer than "overnight," so do not expect your relationship to be normal "overnight" either.

—Diana Ringquist

THE DREADED "D" WORD

Deployment. One of the most dreaded words no spouse wants to hear, but a word that will instill a sense of pride in them regardless! The first thing to do when you get to any installation is find your family. It more than likely will not be your actual family, but find one, or someone you can relate to and create a family away from home.

Even if your spouse is not set to deploy, the chances of them going is always good. Do not live your life like your spouse is going to leave the next day, but it's always good to be prepared for the unknown and having your military family no matter what happens is always a plus.

Having someone to pick your kids up if you have a flat tire, or bring you dinner when everyone in your house has been sick and you just cannot cook another can of chicken noodle soup can be a life saver. Another might be having that person just sit with you in silence while you cry because you miss your spouse so much.

The bills and issues with the car and house can all be fixed but your emotional well-being is the number one priority. Make sure you take care of that first! If you have that then everything else will eventually fall into place.

When your spouse returns, you will have someone to give you time to readjust. The leaving is hard but the return can be hard also, especially if they have been gone for more than six months. That routine you have made is yours and yours only, but remember your spouse has a routine too.

Merging these two routines takes time and patience. Make sure you give it the time it needs. Deployments, TDY, training exercises, whatever, may separate you and your spouse, and doesn't get easier the more times you do it. It may seem that way since you may not cry as much as you did the first time, or your mind is focused on the kids a little more this time, but it does not get easier. You just become more prepared for what's ahead. Take that as a badge of honor!

—*Whitney Messer*

HANDLING REDEPLOYMENT
(IT'S TRICKIER THAN YOU THINK)

Deployments have become a norm in our family's life and there are some things that have worked for us when reintegrating after a deployment. War is unpredictable. Anything, everything, or even nothing can happen to your spouse in just one deployment. Any of those three can bring back a lot of emotional baggage, good and bad.

Each deployment has had its unique challenges and you need to expect anything. I give my spouse space when he comes home so he can decompress and reacclimate to home life. To be honest, he usually gets physically sick after a deployment because his body starts relaxing and his immune system crashes.

I follow his lead; I do not ask him any questions about what happened, he shares what he can and what he wants to share. I do not expect to get all the details and that is okay. If he needs to sit on the couch for two weeks straight to process what has happened, I let him! I do not give him a to-do list within the first month, except for sex . . . that is a must do.

Even though I don't know the details of what my husband has seen, or the things he has had to do, I still try to put myself in his shoes during his transitioning period. Do you have a vacation booked for his immediate return? Rethink it. Can you give him/her at least a week at home away from people and stimulation?

You may be rolling your eyes and thinking, *What about me? I need to decompress from being a single parent, too.* Be upfront about it and verbally explain to your spouse some things you would like to eventually do without the kids, but don't run for the door.

—*Superwoman*

BLANKET POA

A blanket Power of Attorney is a document that allows you to act as your spouse's legal representative when he or she is not available to do so. It is a great document to have even if your spouse is not deployed, because TDYs happen and some days they just cannot leave the office to deal with something.

Talk to legal with your spouse and they can assist you with creating a blanket POA and explain what specific powers you do and do not have. If your spouse is not available and you need to authorize repairs to a vehicle, you need to change your phone plan or provider, you want to change or access bank information, or any number of actions, a blanket POA will allow you to do so.

Make sure you get several *original* copies, as many organizations and companies require an original and not a copy. (As a side note, your spouse can get one for you in case you are not available. It is also a good idea to have one for any non-minor family members you may become responsible for, such as aging parents.)

—*Diana Ringquist*

Author's Note: There are several types of Powers of Attorney, such as General, Durable, and Special. Get legal advice, as it is important to know which one is best for your purposes. For example, some may become ineffective if the person giving POA becomes incapacitated, which may not be what you want.

SET UP SYSTEMS

Systems can be applied to daily life and can include everything from paying bills to whose turn it is to do the dishes to how you arrange your storage. Systems are simply the routines and habits you use to manage your day-to-day, week-to-week, month-to-month daily life. We all know how often we change bedding, who takes out the trash, and when we go grocery shopping. By having systems in place, we free up time to do those things we want to do.

When a person is removed from or introduced to a system for a period of time, the system will almost always get disrupted. It can disrupt money management, cleaning schedules, personal time, daily routines, and can be as simple as not cutting the sandwich diagonally or as significant as running up credit card debt. What remains consistent in system disruption, as Hollywood movies have shown us in hits like *Mr. Mom*, *Daddy Daycare*, and *The Pacifier*, is that it causes stress on everyone involved.

Hopefully, you will read this before a deployment and can work with your service member to set up systems to transition into deployment, during deployment, and return from deployment. Working together can help ease the departures and returns, because your service member will better understand the routines and systems in place. If you are already on your own, let your service member know what you have set up, once you have smoothed out the new system. This way, reentry can be an easier experience for everyone and help limit hurt feelings and misunderstandings.

—*Diana Ringquist*

PART 9

Pets—Do We Have to Flush Goldie?

WAIT FOR KITTY

I am an animal lover. I grew up with pets of all kinds and am used to having animals as part of my family. But I am not used to living this nomad life and moving every couple of years.

I consider myself lucky that my children share my passion for animals and my love for all things furry. But of course that privilege comes with the constant question of, "Mommy, why can't we have a [insert cute pet here]?"

Well:

1. Because I don't need another living creature to lug across the world. Because the thought of adding a pet and their accompanying pet carrier to our plethora of luggage while traversing the airports of the world gives me hives.
2. Because I know that every two years, we will have to put kitty underneath an airplane for countless hours and entrust her safety to complete strangers.
3. Because veterinary care in third world countries is questionable at best and often nonexistent.
4. Because pets add an extra complexity to vacations and we are constantly on the go.
5. Because our assigned housing probably won't have room for a pony.

It's inevitable though, that I know. The addition to our family will come one day because the truth is that I want it as much as the kids do.

Hopefully, I can at least delay it until my wonderful children can carry their own bags so that I can use my newly freed hands to wrangle the fur-baby.

—*Victoria Griffith*

ADOPTION VS. ACCOMPANYING—
MAKING A TOUGH DECISION

Loki had been with us since the start of our relationship. He was a very large, beautiful, usually noble-looking mix of Great Dane, German Shepherd, and Malamute with a thick black coat, crazy-looking brown eyes, and half of his left ear. Most people were intimidated on first sight, but the only fear was that you may trip over him.

Loki was our companion through deployment, guardian helper in raising our children, and constant fixture as we moved from assignment to assignment. He was aging well and was deeply loved.

Then the inevitable happened. We had an assignment that forced us to seriously consider if it would be a good move for Loki. We were headed to a tropical environment in a country where dogs were disliked and occasionally eaten. He would not be able to run freely, likely be shunned by locals, he would have to fly as cargo, and in his aging had begun to have some minor problems with his hips.

Adoption to friends or family members is something you may need to consider before getting a pet, or if you already have one, something to consider if you are faced with an assignment that will not accept or allow your pet.

Some locations have programs in place to help you adopt or foster out your pet. Abandoning your pet is never an acceptable action. Similarly, euthanizing an otherwise healthy pet is equally unacceptable. Talk with your friends and family members in advance about your pet's options. Learn about and support organizations that assist service members and their pets. There may be plenty of people who would jump at a chance to adopt or foster your furry, feathered, finned, and scaly family members.

As for Loki, we were incredibly lucky that we had dear friends who had lost their dog two years prior and lived on a 51-acre farm. Loki adapted to his new family well and was loved and spoiled well beyond his life expectancy. He died peacefully, loved and cared for, as a very old dog.

—*Diana Ringquist*

YOUR GOVERNMENT-ISSUED PETS

The comic Paula Poundstone did a hilarious bit about her excessive pets: "Nine cats, a big stupid dog, a bearded dragon lizard, a bunny, and one ant left from my ant farm."

Sure, that sounds nice. But to save much heartache, and to manage the inevitable moves into government quarters/too small apartments/ places with picky landlords, think very long and hard about each pet you bring into your household. Your dog may appreciate four-legged pals to run around with, and the kids are just crazy about the free ferret being offered in front of Walmart. But government quarters generally have a two-pet rule, and landlords will often limit pets to cats and dogs, if they allow them at all.

There are also weight limits, and breed exclusions. To avoid future problems, stick with no more than a grand total of two non-aggressive breed dogs under 20 to 45 lbs., and/or a domestic cat.

Sure, there are military families with horses, chickens, iguanas, you name it. But they make sacrifices in where they live, usually incurring a hefty commute time and expense. In some situations, you may have no choice but to accept government quarters, or give up your housing allowance. Or worst of all, re-home the pets.

But don't flush Goldie. There's almost always someone around who will adopt aquarium fish.

—*Tracey Enerson Wood*

I'M NOT ABOVE BRIBERY

At twenty-four years of service to the US Air Force, I thought we were done. Done with anticipating the next assignment. Done with the endless research for the right house, in the right school district. Done with the packing and the unpacking.

I thought we were ready to settle down with no more moves and finally get a dog. I was so ready; I even looped the kids into my dreams. Then, on one fateful day, my husband shared his own dream to get back to Europe one more time.

Our journey to Europe involved not one, but two moves. My and the kids' dream of a puppy dissolved into the air, until I discovered my tool of inspiration and persuasion to help us weather this move . . . the dog.

As we orchestrated and maneuvered through our PCS for a ten-month training tour, the groundwork for our future furry friend became not only our fantasy, but our fuel, to survive the craziness, the insecurity, the excitement, and the frustration of living like nomads.

Vidar, our Norwegian Pup

Our future dog calmed anxious hearts, dried sad eyes, and lifted deflated spirits. "Future Dog" brought excitement and hope. He or she also brought parental leverage when the minions of the house (a.k.a. the children) became a bit rebellious at the thought of moving—again.

Once we arrived in Norway, the search was on. I became obsessed, but my obsession paid off and the perfect dog for us joined our crew.

LIFE HACK

Sometimes extreme methods of appeasing the kids will keep them excited and add to life's adventures!

—*Jenn Steffens*

PET RECORDS

"We arrived at the kennel where our pet was going to stay while we're on vacation, and they turned us away! Apparently, we didn't have the right shots needed to board."

"I can't believe it! Our connecting flight got cancelled and we are stuck in Lisbon overnight. Our pets don't have permission to enter the EU! What are we going to do?"

"Let me get this right. You are telling me that because of HIPAA, you can't give me a copy of my pet's medical records without my pet's consent. Really?"

It can be argued that keeping your pet records up to date is more important than keeping your family's medical records up to date. Military medical and dental facilities and civilian medical and dental practices in the United States are either linked or have developed very good methods of sharing records with your permission. Depending on where you are going, this may not be enough and paper copies or originals are required.

When you are stationed outside the United States, you are given guidance and reminders about how to ensure your medical records are provided to your next assignment. Handling your pet's health history and medical records is less clearly defined and can vary greatly from place to place.

Your last veterinarian may send you reminders, but they can take extra time catching up to you post-move, and not all practices send reminders. There are apps and calendars available to help you remember your pet's vaccination and check-ups. These are helpful as you juggle the rest of the demands of moving your life and the lives of your family from place to place.

As with your personal medical records, you can request the physical records from your veterinarian. It may take some explaining as to why you need them, but generally practices are willing to provide them. Check with your new assignment to find out what documents you will need to provide before, during, and after the move. Airlines, states, and countries all have their own rules and regulations.

Whether you are passing through or staying there, you may be held to specific requirements that can derail your move if you're unprepared. Ask those at your next assignment what is required. Contact local veterinarians where you will be stationed if possible, to see if they are taking new patients and to confirm the records required. Check online for prepared, printable pet record forms and do some research as to what is required for your trip. It is better to be over-prepared than take a chance.

—*Diana Ringquist*

PET TRANSPORTATION

"I'm settled in my seat and I look out the window only to see four ground crew guys chasing my dog across the tarmac!"

"What do you mean we can't take our pet on this flight? We paid for and received a ticket for him!"

"Our pets are getting much better at long drives. One only vomits three or four times and the other one gets exhausted from constant crying after about seven hours!"

Whether you move your animals yourself, pay a company to move them, or have the sometimes-challenging experience of flying them, transporting your pets is always interesting.

Think about what is best for your pet and for you. Build your plans from that point. Consider how you will be getting to your next home, how your pet will get there, what costs and paperwork may be involved, how long the trip will be, what supplies and equipment you will need, and how much you are willing to be directly involved with your pet in the move.

Driving across the United States may sound fun, exciting, or even romantic. Driving across the United States with an eleven-year-old, a two-year-old, a large dog, a remarkably loud and opinionated cat, several suitcases, and the three racing bikes on the roof rack of a Mazda 5 while your military member has just a few suitcases in his Prius and cannot understand why you "can't keep up" pretty much kills that illusion. The in-car food fight broke out about an hour from our destination and somehow saved my sanity!

—*Diana Ringquist*

FREEDOM IN THE POTOMAC

Here we are again. After nearly ten months of living in Alexandria, Virginia, we are on the move again, this time to Norway. Our twin seven-year-old boys enjoyed the company of their betta fish, Kevin and Mr. Fantail. We were now at the stage of what to do with the fish.

I promised—okay, I somewhat—okay, maybe I didn't try to find new homes for these anti-social gilled critters. I had a few other things to do on my list, and truthfully, I forgot all about the fish right up until a few days before we were due to leave.

I found my inspiration on my daily walking path along the Potomac River. Oh, the possibilities! The excitement and thrill of being a beautiful betta fish set free in a quasi-clean river!

We are not sure how long Kevin and Mr. Fantail endured their new habitat, but our boys found comfort that at least their aquatic buddies had freedom, even if it was found in the bottom link of the food chain.

LIFE HACK

There is always a science lesson in every situation.

—*Jenn Steffens*

Author's Note: Be sure to check environmental regulations before placing non-native fish into local waters.

PET CONSIDERATIONS

A pet is a part of the family, and when it comes time to move, that needs to be taken into deep consideration, depending on where you are going. Here is some quick advice: *do not* get a pet if you are not willing to pay the extra fees or go the extra miles to get that pet to the next location!

Moving with a pet takes planning. You must be prepared for a possible quarantine in certain areas or boarding if there isn't a hotel that will allow them. They are great family members but not something you can just throw away because the stress is too much to move with! You can purchase a stuffed animal look-alike online that can be at your door in two days.

—Whitney Messer

PART 10

Living OCONUS
(see Part 1, Annoying Acronyms)

(USUALLY) THE BEST DINNER STORIES!

Living OCONUS is an adventure! It is also at times frustrating, frightening, stressful, dull, exciting, and average. You have the opportunity to do something most people in the world will never get to do: you get to live in another culture!

Do not stay insulated in your home. Get out and explore, engage, try, watch, listen, and do what you can to participate in your host nation within safety guidelines. The good and even the bad experiences will give you stories to share for years to come, even if some are not so great right this minute. No matter what, you will never be the same person and sharing your adventures with others will be a pastime you can all enjoy for years to come.

One point of advice: bring short and high heels for those ever-changing backyard or embassy functions. One time the Deputy Chief of Mission and I shared stories of high heels sinking into deep, well-watered grass. Another time it was a fifteen-minute swarm of fruit bats passing over the party, forcing us to shelter inside while the bats "lightened their load" for their nightly flight.

—*Diana Ringquist*

APPLIANCE DUMPING

On a beautiful spring evening, my future husband and I were discussing all of the items we would ask the movers to pack up and send to his new duty station in Germany. As we checked out all of his furniture and appliances there were a couple things I said *had to go—* as in be thrown out—hopefully never to be seen again.

One of these items was his prized 1970ish used-to-be-white toaster oven. You couldn't even see through the glass door it was so stained and charred. No way, in my mind, was this ancient appliance going to be able to run on the euro plugs. He briefly fought me on it, but conceded and he tossed it.

Well, now married, when we arrived in Germany, being the wonderful new wife that I thought I was, I immediately sought after a brand-spankin'-new, and probably "fancier," European toaster oven. I figured since the Europeans surely know how to make the best bread in the world, that they of course would know how to make amazing toast . . .

Well, I figured wrong. First off, they don't really sell toaster ovens. They sell the two- or four-slice plain toasters, but not toaster ovens. This was not good, since at the time, one of my husband's favorite things was mini breakfast pizzas! So I had to find an oven he could cook them in.

Eventually I gave up on the European market, and I went to our Post Exchange. I looked at their toaster ovens, and of course because we were overseas, they only had a couple stocked. I chose the nicest one, and crossed my fingers this would be good enough. However, when put to use, it was a total failure. I, of course, got the "I told you so" response from the hubster, but being so fed up with looking at toaster ovens, we decided to stick with it through our three years being stationed there.

Our lesson learned was: don't throw out something just because you think it might not work in an overseas duty station. Most modern gadgets are "dual voltage"—meaning they work on both American and European current, and you don't need to do anything more than pack a few inexpensive plug adapters.

It will almost certainly be cheaper than buying all new hair dryers, toasters, blenders, heaters, etc. while in Europe, only to throw those out and buy new again when you return back from overseas.

Do be sure to check the voltage, however. Don't try to run a 110v appliance on 220v with just a plug adapter. You need a voltage transformer.

—Allison Wood

KNOW WHAT YOU ARE SIGNING, IN ENGLISH OR ANY OTHER LANGUAGE

Imagine walking to your mailbox with your coffee in hand, on an unsuspecting Tuesday morning. You open your mailbox not to find a greeting card, coupons, or even a bill, but a collection notice! What? You're a responsible adult. What is happening? Did you forget to pay a bill? Did someone open a credit card in your name? Did your husband buy a boat and not tell you? No. The European telephone company and a partnering US collection agency have found you stateside, months after your trek back to the United States, asking for 1,200 Euro to collect on a cell phone service debt that you do not even owe! How did we get to this point?

There are many adjustments to moving overseas, but the biggest one I found was how many foreign countries still operate on a hand receipt system when you make utility or services payments. The process while in Europe was to walk into the physical location to pay your bill. Your payment is taken, and a receipt given back to you. It seems simple enough. But once you make your payment and collect your receipt, you can't tell if the company's employee recorded the amount paid in their records.

That is how my husband and I landed in our collection situation. Month after month, our payment was taken, but never recorded. So over time, the initial amount of the "supposed" debt was compounded along with finder's and collection fees, reaching us in the United States, months later. Thank goodness my husband and I had learned to be pack rats when it comes to bills and important documents. Our record-keeping saved us! We had documentation of every payment made on the contract allowing us, ultimately, to be relinquished of any debt owed.

The single, most useful piece of advice I can offer you is to prevent locking yourself into any telephone or service contract at any foreign duty station. If it is avoidable, *do not do it*! If you must sign a contract, always ask questions. Sometimes when English is a second language, things can be misinterpreted. Do not leave the conversation until all parties are on the same page. It's okay if you annoy the store or services clerk. It's their job to help you. If you are the least bit hesitant or uncomfortable, walk away and come back the next day after sleeping on it, or get a second opinion altogether. It may be a little inconvenient to buy a prepaid SIM card or telephone service minutes, but it will save you time and hassle on the back end. No one needs to fight a language barrier collection battle if at all avoidable! Think smart and be resourceful to set yourself up for success while overseas!

LIFE HACK

Make an OCONUS business folder.

—Stephanie Dobson

Author's Note: Yes! You will be tracked down and responsible for debts, even if you don't believe you owe them. Also be aware that in many foreign countries, you must give many months of advance notice for discontinuing contracts.

PICTURE DICTIONARIES AND CHARADES

There is no guarantee you will receive any language training before you land in your OCONUS country. You may find that the host nation locals speak English well, and/or you live in a large military community where English is all you really need to get around.

You may also find that you are the only English speaker in the room or on your street. Either way, learning another language changes the way you look at the world and demonstrates to your host nation companions that you care.

When learning a new language, start by ignoring all the other Americans who tell you the language is "easy" or "simple" to learn. It's okay if you struggle learning a new language—the point is that you're trying!

Accept that you may be "childlike" in your language capacity regardless of how well you know the language. Local expressions and inflections may differ from what you learned.

Be ready to smile and laugh at yourself when you make a mistake. This skill puts everyone at ease and others will often work that much harder to help you learn. Finally, when all else fails, a child's picture dictionary gives you the ability to point at what you want and a little bit of charades can usually communicate what you need.

—Diana Ringquist

NOT ALL OCONUS POSTS ARE EQUAL

I stopped reading my friend's post after, "I can't find my favorite brand of . . ." I didn't need to know what favorite brand she couldn't find. Whatever it was, the item she needed was there in some form—she lived in Europe, for crying out loud!

At the time, I was living in West Africa, a country that I enjoyed tremendously, but the sentence of "I can't find . . ." was followed by an extensive list of entire categories of items I had foolishly assumed would be available: flour, milk, cheese, beef, baking powder, cereal, on and on. The next West African country we lived in had all these items and more. When we moved to Europe, I bemoaned the fact that I could not find my "favorite brand" of West African items.

To your family and friends, living OCONUS may seem exotic and exciting. Where you live OCONUS will determine what you have access to and can purchase or enjoy. The reality is that it is still living life. Try to focus less on the lack and more on the new and alternative.

Remember that your inconvenience is a bump in the road and when you do find your "favorite brand of," be grateful and enjoy it more fully. No place is perfect, but your attitude makes all the difference. I am still upset that I cannot find Teem soda anywhere in the United States!

—*Diana Ringquist*

EXPLORE LOCAL CUISINE

Commissaries (or post/base grocery stores) are one of the benefits available to those who serve overseas. They provide fresh, convenient, and reliable food at affordable prices.

However, they can also lead to a missed opportunity to experience an integral part of all cultures—the cuisine! Sometimes Americans can get stuck in what is comfortable and familiar, a trait that is almost certainly then passed down to children.

Sometimes when you're in a faraway land, you just want your favorite treats, to bring you home with familiar tastes and aromas, if only for one meal. That is perfectly understandable and even necessary sometimes. But a lot of the time it's just as important to branch out and learn about the culture, foods, and ingredients of your temporarily adopted land. Isn't that one of the many gifts military life has to offer?

Although it can be overwhelming, do shop at local markets. Ask friends from the local area for their favorite recipes they grew up on. In my experience, people are always willing and proud to share their heritage. If you're feeling shy, the Internet is an easy resource with recipes even for those less handy in the kitchen.

LIFE HACK

Get out of your comfort zone and enjoy where you are!
You won't regret it.

—*Kristen Riffle*

PARENTING IS A DIFFERENT BALL GAME OVERSEAS

Most of us are quite comfortable with the world we grew up in. The country that we call home. The place where we know the traditions and understand the culture. But what happens when you are propelled into a land unknown? You often don't speak the language and no amount of research can prepare you for the reality of day-to-day living.

For us, we were moving to a ". . . stan" which already caused a panicked spiral because the region is so incredibly different than the home we knew.

We were told about daily life, briefed on traditions, and did some of our own research and we thought we knew what to expect.

The first culture shock was the air quality. We weren't expecting the dust, the sand, and the pollution. We had to learn how to live with the windows closed, with air purifiers and humidifiers running around the clock. We had to figure out how to explain to the toddler that she couldn't play outside today because "the air is dirty."

The second lifestyle change was not having drinkable water. Anywhere. We were lucky enough to have a house that was fitted with enough levels of filtration to clean even the most toxic sludge. But that did not apply to restaurants or anywhere beyond our walls. So bottled water it was (and that was not always trustworthy).

One thing we learned was that filters that strip water of the bad, often also strip water of the good—leaving you with dead water. It took dizziness and lethargy for us to figure this out. Electrolyte replacement drinks became part of our daily diet to replace what we were missing.

Markets, markets everywhere! I was so excited to be able to have fresh fruit and vegetables and make wonderful salads. What I was not aware of was that all of this beautiful produce was grown in land watered with the same contaminated water that was running through the pipes. Hence, contaminated produce. So now in order to make those wonderful salads I first had to soak everything in a vinegar solution.

I had to explain to the toddler that she couldn't just eat the apple that the wonderful lady at the market gave her because she could get sick.

Parenting is also a very different ball game in different parts of the world, from the way we think kids should be raised, to the things that we believe babies can or cannot do and/or have, wear, or eat.

As a Westerner, I'm quite used to having my own personal space. I'm used to people respecting my boundaries and my parenting choices. And if they don't, they at least try keep their opinions to themselves, or have the decency to share their opinions behind my back and not add to the already huge mountain of mom guilt.

But in this new home I found myself constantly fending off well-meaning ladies who just wanted to pet and kiss my beautiful little girl. When they weren't trying to touch, they were kindly handing her treats. Teeth-breaking, choking-hazard kinds of treats. Hard candy was constantly being given to my child who did not yet have a full mouth of teeth and the choking risk was very real. What a mean mom I looked like, always trying to wrestle a sugary morsel away from my screaming baby!

And lastly, when it's October, it's fall. It's almost winter. It may still be warm enough to play outside and even work up a sweat, but you are failing at parenting if your sweating, playing child is not dressed for the middle of winter, including a hat. And boy did the locals let you know!

So just when you are figuring out life in your motherland, living OCONUS throws a whole new set of challenges your way. Stay strong and do your best. You'll be an even better parent when you're back home.

—Victoria Griffith

DELIVERY BY SKYPE

There I was, 31 weeks pregnant with twin boys in Misawa, Japan, with only a level one hospital that did not deliver multiples, and a husband on deployment. My options: head to the Stork's Nest, a special unit for expectant moms at Kadena Air Base in Okinawa for the duration of my pregnancy and stay for several weeks afterward due to the probability of a NICU stay for one or both of the babies, or go back to the United States and move in with family.

Being that we had a five-year-old daughter, adult supervision was legally required. Off to the United States we went to have

the boys! I boarded a rotater flight to head to Georgia to bunk in with my in-laws and be surrounded by all of our family. Thankfully on the flight my fellow passengers included one of my OB doctors, several labor and delivery nurses, and half of the fire department!

For five weeks I was loved, pampered, and cared for by family and friends. My new doctor and I planned the twin's arrival with my husband. He would be with us throughout the delivery on Skype.

Our plan worked! I delivered our boys at 36 weeks, with their dad witnessing the miracle of birth with the help of modern technology. The boys and their dad eventually met each other when we all reunited back in Japan when they were two months old. Happy, healthy, and so very grateful!

LIFE HACK

Be creative with all of your resources!

—*Jenn Steffens*

THANKSGIVING

Year 1: "Can we host Thanksgiving for fifteen of my friends?"
"Yes. I can do that."

Year 2: "Can we host Thanksgiving for twenty-one of my friends?"
"Hmm. I guess I can do that."

Year 3: "How many can I invite this year? Is thirty-two too many?"
Unrecorded amount of silence. "I guess we can make it work . . ."

Everything that makes a traditional, mouth-watering Thanksgiving is hard to come by in a country where turkeys are only sold in a few stores, stuffing cubes and cranberry sauce just doesn't exist, corn is definitely subpar, the oven is the size of my head, and refrigerators are tantamount to a college dorm fridge.

But how do you say "no" to a teenage boy who wants to share one of our greatest traditions and a group of growing friends who want to partake in it?

Simple. You don't. You look to Walmart, the EAA store, friends, and you simply draw on your own creativity (and sanity) to make it work. My saving grace living overseas has been Walmart! Canned cranberry sauce and boxed stuffing which, get this, have a recipe on how to cook it in the crockpot, are two staples I have ordered every year (provided I remembered to order them at least three weeks before Thanksgiving). I do break the bank and order my turkeys through the EAA store, but how many I order is a crapshoot.

Not only is the annual teenage Thanksgiving an event, but we also host a traditional Thanksgiving for my husband's local coworkers, and there's been the occasional extra Thanksgiving for non-American friends who want to see what all the hype is about.

In year three of our tour, I ordered seven turkeys. Two 11–14 pounds (the absolute max that will fit into my dwarf-sized oven), two 8–10 pounds, and three turkey breasts (as back up). Thank you, EAA store! But storage became a nightmare. One turkey barely fit in the fridge with all the other food needed for the feast, so I grabbed the big cooler we brought with us and defrosting the turkeys outside (or inside depending on how cold it was) worked like a charm.

If prepping for thirty-two kids isn't enough, I like the added stress of my slow-cook method, taking three times as long to cook a turkey. Working backwards, I plan the exact moments the turkeys finish, when to prepare the next one, and the exact moment I need to get the first in the oven. It's actually a work of art (one I should have framed).

With the alarms set to keep the turkey rotations going, the next thing to figure out is how to keep all the meat safe and juicy. One trick I learned is to pour gravy over the turkey and store it in the fridge. Then put it in the warmer (see below) about an hour before serving.

The next miracle came from the attaché department at the embassy. I thought I had died and gone to heaven when my friend told me she had a warmer. What bliss I had found! This allowed me to cook multiple things and keep them warm before serving—a true lifesaver! I miss my American-sized fridges (yes, I had two) and oven, but with a little creativity, some loaners from the embassy, the ability to order from Walmart and the EAA store, hosting a big Thanksgiving every year in a country where nothing is big has created memories to last a lifetime.

Year 4: "Can I invite forty people to Thanksgiving this year?"

[Quick text to make sure the warmer is available.] "Definitely. Wouldn't think about not doing it."

—*Stacey Benzing*

DON'T FORGET YOUR FIRE EXTINGUISHER

My husband called me with two choices: small, furnished, right outside the Hill 180 Gate (What the heck is that?!) or large, unfurnished, not close to base. I opted for the first choice, which would become our off-base home on his unaccompanied tour at Osan AFB, South Korea.

It was my first time over an ocean and I'd quit my job, put our belongings in storage, and bought a ticket to Seoul. I arrived on a dark, snowy day in January of 2001. My husband had booked a room in a gorgeous hotel for the weekend. Korea was beautiful and exciting. Then the weekend was over. I could tell he was hesitating to show me our new home. Finally, he had no choice.

I still search for words to describe what was waiting for me. Our neighborhood was crowded, the streets tiny, our neighbor was a drunken dog breeder—the kind sold for food. The smell, my goodness, the smell!

Our apartment was above the landlord, Mr. Kim. His wife was sweet and filled the house with daily Buddhist chants and the aroma of fish cakes. It was warm, cozy, and completely bizarre. It had a tiny bathtub, non-existent water pressure, and stick-figure instructions on how to use the toilet. There were bars on the windows and exposed wire everywhere.

Mr. Kim worked for Civil Engineering at the base and prided himself on providing a "dual voltage" home. He specifically gave us a fire extinguisher to sleep with next to our bed, just in case the wires were to set fire. Despite all the wackiness of that apartment and year, we treasure our memories of, hopefully, once-in-a-lifetime experiences.

LIFE HACK

Roll with it, it will be a wild, but lovely ride!

—*Jenn Steffens*

HOW TO FIND A BEAUTICIAN

When we got stationed in Korea, I had no idea what bathroom meant in Korean, no less grocery store, no less what hair salon was! However, after living there a couple of weeks I was in frantic need of a new perm. It's all I could think about! In desperation I finally figured out what "hair salon" was in Korean and booked an appointment at the closest salon off the base.

Perms were the in thing to do back then too, so no judging! I figured a hair salon right off base would have decent experience treating different types of hair. Boy, did I figure wrong.

First off, they put on a lot more perm solution then I was used to (probably needed for thicker hair, compared to my northern European thin hair) and then left it in curlers for way too long. I walked out of there looking more like a poodle than the Dolly Parton golden locks I had imagined. Make that a torched poodle.

As a more experienced spouse and traveler, I have now learned to simply just approach anyone you see around base who has a hair style/cut that you like the look of, and ask them where they go to get their hair done! Works every time.

—Lesley Gagnon

WHEN YOUR TV CATCHES FIRE

There is a distinct, unforgettable, and difficult to describe sound that happens when a 110v television is plugged into a 220v outlet by mistake. The smell of the ensuing fire and the sight of flames licking up the inside of the screen is equally unforgettable and difficult to describe.

"Holy Crap! Get out of there! Get *out of there!*" I yelled at my (then) 14-year-old who was helping me set up our television and all the accompanying equipment. Fear gripped my heart as time slowed and my child seemed to move as if the air had become Jell-O. In reality, it could not have been more than half a heartbeat for my child to get out from behind the TV and credenza, cover the space between us, and stand behind me with hands on my waist as I prepared to slay this now fire-breathing, smoke-belching appliance.

Know where you are going, whether they have 110v or 220v, the kind of outlet adapter you may need, and if transformers are provided or not. Small appliances that have moving parts (blenders, for example) or heat up (hair dryers and such) are particularly prone to an early death in the transformer world. You may want to buy a 220v version.

Check your appliances and electronics first, as many on the market can handle both voltages. Even if they can, many countries have power surges and/or failures that can harm your item. Arm yourself with an armful of inexpensive surge protector power strips. Remember to write the date you begin using your surge protector on the protector as they should not be used more than two years at most, as the protection part is likely to be damaged or burned out. Electrical fires are no joke. Be vigilant!

As for my television, I unplugged the transformer from the wall and the fire went out, and thankfully no damage had been done to anything else. Now, I strongly recommend against what I did next. I plugged the TV into the correct transformer outlet and plugged in the transformer, ready to pull the plug if my child, who was monitoring from a safe distance, reported further flames. With confirmation that all was well, I grabbed the remote and turned the TV on, flipping through the channels. It worked fine, except that it was slow to "warm up" and show a picture, and said picture would go from color to black and white every so often. My housekeeper discovered that this was easily remedied by changing the channel and then changing it back again. We did turn the transformer off and unplug it when not in use.

Also, be at least passingly familiar with the differences between standard and metric measurements. A kilometer, for example is 0.62 miles. Imagine my excitement and subsequent disappointment when I, a slow runner at an 11-minute mile, completed a kilometer in just 6 minutes! Go ahead and do the math. I'll wait.

—Diana Ringquist

THE CALENDAR

Another humorous London incident was when someone invited me to go grab a drink. I had started using the British term for a calendar, which is "diary." But then, remembering I was actually talking to another American, I tried midway to switch. I said, "I'd love to join; I just have to check my diary-uhhhh-calendar and get back to you."

Confused, she responded, "Umm—you have a diarrhea calendar . . .??" Needless to say, I was slightly mortified.

> ## LIFE HACK
>
> Mixing cultures in conversations can lead to embarrassing moments. Slow down, think it through before you open your mouth.

—Kristen Riffle

GO-BAGS, GRAB-BAGS, AND SHELTER-IN-PLACE: NOT JUST FOR PREPPERS ANYMORE

The concepts of a "Go-bag" (also called a "bug-out bag"), a "Grab-bag," and "Shelter-in-place" preparations may seem silly or even "out-there," but they are an essential part of your OCONUS (and in modern times, CONUS) life. These are essential parts of disaster preparedness and crisis management. Weather events, social and political unrest, disease spread, or family emergency can all be made easier if you are prepared with some basics.

There are numerous resources online and within our military and foreign service communities that address the concepts of what should be included in these bags. Once you've prepared them, set a reminder to go through them every six months or so, to determine if the supplies are still appropriate (kids grow, products expire, records need updating).

A "Go-bag" should be prepared and kept for every member of the family, and include pets. "Shelter-in-place" plans need to account for everyone in the family and pets and be modified as needed as your family changes due to life events, TDYs, and deployments. For items that you need on a daily basis (driver's licenses, work and school IDs, beloved toys), create a specific list that you keep with your bags so you can gather them quickly if needed.

—*Diana Ringquist*

WHEN THE LIGHTS (AND EVERYTHING ELSE) GO OUT

"You can always tell the new kids at school," my high school freshman announced. "They're the ones that stop working and look around when the power goes out. The rest of us just keep right on going."

Power failures happen. Depending on where you are in the world, they can happen several times a day, every day. There are a myriad of products available on the market to help you deal with these situations. Consider what you will need before you buy.

Computers and other electronics should have a UPS (Uninterrupted Power Source). These are large and often heavy devices that contain a power surge protector and battery. It plugs into the wall, then you plug your electronic devices into it to protect them from power surges and keep them going when the power goes out.

Pay attention when you are considering purchasing a UPS. Be certain that the UPS can be plugged into the power supply at your new assignment. That means check the type of power it's rated for (220v, 110v, or dual voltage) and what kind of plug it will need. Often UPS devices will not work if you try to use them with transformers or adapters.

Power transformers are supplied at some assignments, but there never seem to be enough. Ask if you will need a power transformer at your new assignment. Find out if they are available where you are going and how much they cost. If you are told they are supplied, ask how many are given to each family. Depending on the answers, you may want to purchase some before your pack out.

Alternative power source supplies and devices: While battery operated devices are good, you need to be able to get batteries and that can be a struggle in some parts of the world. Consider purchasing a collection of solar, hand-cranked, and similar items. These may include lights, power packs, radios and televisions, and more. Shop around, talk to people already living at your new assignment, and remember source diversity is important. The sun may not always shine brightly enough or long enough, the wind may not blow, you may not be near running water, and there is only so long one can crank a handle to get enough charge.

—*Diana Ringquist*

LOST IN TRANSLATION

One of the most fun and interesting aspects of living overseas, especially in a country that also uses English as their mother tongue, is the subtle but significant difference in the language. A small turn of phrase can lead to confusion or even unintentional insult.

One occasion this happened to me was when we were living in London. I had gotten to know some of my neighbors, and we always said "hello," and a bit of small talk when we encountered each other. A few times the women who owned our flat would see me in the morning, while I was hurrying to drop off my three kids at school.

She would ask, "Are you alright!?"

A bit ruffled, I would respond, "Yes, we're just fine." *Of course I'm okay, I just probably look a bit rough and frazzled dealing with these American troll children first thing in the morning! Thanks for noticing!*

But as I lived there longer and heard the greeting more and more, I realized it's just the British way of saying, "Hey, how are you?" with absolutely zero comment on your physical appearance or well-being, good or bad. No need to think others are concerned for you.

LIFE HACK

Be aware of different meanings in other English-speaking countries.

—*Kristen Riffle*

About the Authors

Kristen Riffle is a seasoned military family member and spouse. Growing up as an army brat, she had a brief glimpse into the civilian world at Virginia Tech. That fling ended when she married a fellow VT graduate, who then became a naval officer. She has spent her entire life traveling the world, but currently calls Oslo, Norway, home, where she lives with her husband, four kids, a corgi, and a giant Norwegian Forest kitten.

She has experience as a content writer for the DoD family programs. She has many hobbies and passions in addition to writing, traveling, healthy cooking from scratch, and volunteering at her kids' schools. She considers herself lucky to have a transient military lifestyle, meeting all the incredible people along the way and is always awaiting the next adventure!

Allison Wood is a mother of four and Army Explosive Ordnance Disposal spouse of seven years. Born into a military family, she has a lifetime of experience adjusting to new environments, seeking new opportunities, and making new friends.

A salesperson at heart, she's sold labor, lumber, and MLB Baseball tickets to great effect (or like a boss!). She's been a college basketball athlete, a triathlete, and was a fitness instructor for a decade. Currently, her many passions include serving her local community and church in several roles focusing on working with children as a worship leader and teacher. She spends her free time maintaining a tenuous grasp on sanity and accidentally falling asleep.

Tracey Enerson Wood has always had a writing bug. While working as a registered nurse, starting her own interior design company, raising two children, and bouncing around the world as a military wife, she indulged in her passion as a playwright, screenwriter, and novelist. She has authored magazine columns and other nonfiction, written and directed plays of all lengths, including  *Grits, Fleas, and Carrots*; *Rocks and Other Hard Places*; *Alone*, and *Fog*. Her screenplays include "Strike Three" and "Roebling's Bridge."

Other passions include food and cooking, and honoring military heroes. She is also the co-author of *Homefront Cooking: Recipes, Wit, and Wisdom from American Veterans and Their Loved Ones*, which was released by Skyhorse Publishing in May 2018, and all authors' profits are donated to organizations that support veterans. Her novel, *The Engineer's Wife*, was released by Sourcebooks in April 2020. She lives with her family in Florida.

Her author website is tracey enersonwood.com.

Kaitlin Walsh was an Air Force wife; her husband served for eight years. She is now an independent artist specializing in abstract anatomy watercolors. From a young age, she exhibited an immense fascination with both art and science. She focused her studies on both disciplines, taking medical courses alongside fine art ones. This culminated with a graduate degree in Biomedical Visualization at the University of Illinois at Chicago. Kaitlin feels incredibly lucky to find success doing what she loves while getting to spend time with her family.

More of her story and art can be seen at lyonroadart.com.

Acknowledgments

And a huge, heartfelt thanks to all our story contributors for being willing to share their expertise: Stacey Benzing; Staci-Jill Burnley, Army Logistics spouse; Jessi Burns, Army wife of 18 years; Diane Campbell, spouse, Army (retired); Heather Murphy Capps, Northern Virginia, is a teacher, writer, and former television news reporter who can attest to the fact that life hacks and a sense of humor are an indispensable part of being an Army wife; Jackie Cooper; Olivia Devescovi; Stephanie Dobson, Villa Rica, Georgia; Susie ·Doyle, St. Petersburg, Florida; Katie Elze, Army wife of 15 years, mom to 2 girls (11 and 5 years old), currently living in Stuttgart, Germany; Bob Enerson, Richmond, Virginia; Meredith Farington; Lesley Gagnon, 17-year Army Cavalry spouse; GamGam, Navy (retired) spouse, and Navy (active duty) mom; Victoria Griffith; Yvette Hulsman; Katie Landis, military wife of 8 years, mom of 2 girls and 1 Great Dane, professional pre-move purger; Jessica Lindville; Whitney Messer, military spouse, 9 years US Army, 3 years US Air Force (and still going); Diana Ringquist; Meredith Rummel; Jenn Steffens; Karissa Sylvester; Carol Van Drie, Okemos, Michigan; and Lauren Walsh.